Traces of a Life

BRAD DREW

Traces of a Life

MARKS & MUSINGS
IN POETRY & IMAGES 1966 – 2020
REVISED & UPDATED

PREFACE TO THE REVISED EDITION

Five years have passed since the production of the First Edition of 'Traces of a Life' and in that time, the world has further changed and in this moment, its future appears uncertain and hangs in some sort of biological, social and economic limbo.

A few older poems have been unearthed, to be re-examined; and, since they carry the stamp of their age in the milieu where they had their genesis, I felt that their eventual inclusion was warranted; even though I might myself, regard them critically now, they were a fitting response to those years.

During these past five years, many new poems have managed to make their way into the light of day and I feel they show a continuing development in approach and style in most instances. In extending this volume, as it were at both extremities, I feel justified in revisiting much of its underlying structure, to reformat it in some respects of overall layout and design. The core content will remain essentially the same but with some adjustment in places, of the illustrations and, in all probability, the inclusion of some new artwork.

This present time of worldwide retreat and entrenchment seems an apt moment to be finally turning to this exercise of re-presenting my own meanderings and I trust the reader will find some pleasure in the result.

Brad Drew
10th of April, 2020

FOREWARD

Brad Drew traces his earlier life abroad, and his later Australian experience, in various poetic forms.

Initially, in the Japanese forms of the tanka and haiku; later, his poems reach out to us through more familiar English forms, such as sonnets and villanelles.

Brad's love of family is also reflected in his many drawings of family and friends, as well as in various scenes.

Many poems here, muse upon the cost, as well as the pleasures, of loving. The pain of loss and the disturbance of absence are clearly expressed. These too, are enhanced by Brad's artwork, accompanying many poems.

Bruce Dawe AO
(15 February 1930 – 01 April 2020)

11 February 2016

INTRODUCTION

I grew up with books as favourite companions, in genres which became increasingly eclectic in their distribution; but I do not recall having any particular interest in poetry per se during my primary or secondary, nor even my tertiary, education years.

I was the first child, and the only boy, in a brood of four siblings; and as such, had the good fortune to receive three years of my mother's undivided attention. Some of my earliest memories, visually strong down to the details of home and furnishings, are of being held on her lap while she read to me. When the distraction of my first sister arrived, I was to a degree, prepared in having a small library of my own; admittedly picture-books in the main, with their few words already committed to memory: pop-up and layered, see-through books, such as one treasured copy of Charles Kingsley's 'The Water Babies'. Come primary school, the library continued to grow, with Enid Blyton's 'Famous Five' reigning supreme, along with Richard Crompton's 'William' books, and some boy called 'Jennings', by Anthony Buckeridge; all of this lot alongside a 'Treasury of Science' and eventually, "The Supernatural Omnibus': a collection of short stories from many of the classic writers (perhaps the first classics I had ever read; though somewhere in earlier times, there had been various copies of Classics Comics), all in one weighty volume – short stories to send a chill, just before bed ... So passed my early youth.

Later, during my secondary school years, the study of set texts overshadowed much of my reading for pure pleasure; which in itself, had moved into a general interest in matters like psychology and hypnosis, science and geology. Not all was questing curiosity though: at school, there was the first experience and enjoyment of Shakespeare; in private, there came the discovery of the better, classic science fiction of those times, alongside the likes of Agatha Christie and Ion Idriess.

University years followed along similar lines, although the scope of extracurricular reading matter became increasingly eclectic, in both fictional and factual content ... but still, poetry for its own sake, remained an uncharted territory.

I suppose it was only within the lyrics of some of the more soulful, romantic, even depressive, popular singer-songwriters around the turning over from the sixties into the seventies, that I found some impetus to express myself in verse. This of course, was prompted by the appearance of a certain girl who captured my heart totally at that time. Romantic interests were nothing new but this was more than noteworthy. Perhaps it was just the timing, perhaps it was in fact, the girl. Whatever it was, she was the catalyst who swept me in her wake, to London and gave birth to an active interest in poetry. I never saw her again; and the poetry, in retrospect, was naive, raw and embarrassingly laden with the obvious influence of some of those songwriters.

However, the poetry was now in my life as fact and what eventually followed in those London years, saw a very tangible development in its overall growth in that city. Inevitably there came about in London, another brief encounter: a girl who was to smoulder quietly in the background of my life for the next twenty-five-odd years, with the occasional random reappearance ... but the poetry making and reading of it, had already taken on its own life and was now was established as a life-long presence secure in its own right.

* * * * *

One of my fellow poets makes reference to 'cathartic process in high emotional times', as one generator in her poetic process. It goes without saying, that owning the characteristics of the perennial romantic, has also a definite advantage. I have no doubt that somewhere in this process, lies the genesis of many a poet ... if not most. Once experienced, the joy of the process itself takes over; and who has never experienced the immediacy of the need to respond to that late-night or early hours visit from the muse, rather than risk chancing that unattended line or phrase, to dissolution in the morning light?

Another of my peers, echoes a core belief of mine, that "poetry should be read aloud". This may seem obvious but not necessarily so, by the evidence one sometimes encounters, masquerading as 'poetry'. The breaking-up of a piece of personal diatribe, a shopping list or even ordinary prose, into manipulated lines where, no matter how creative on paper the arrangement may look, it will rarely of itself, convincingly succeed as a credible poem; likewise, at the same time, unconstrained diatribe, however nobly-perceived the cause, remains just that.

Conversely, some of our best prose, in itself manages to contain more poetry than many 'poets' could ever hope to conjure. In whatever sphere one's poetic leanings might lie, the acid test comes with an aural rendering of the work; and the line of distinction can often appear tenuous, even arguable, as performance artists strive to coerce that shopping list or telephone directory into resounding with high drama.

Whatever the content or aim of a poem might be, it is not just in the words chosen but, most-importantly, the simple ordering of those words, (irrespective of the relative plainness or erudition of the language used), where the magic which sets it apart from its fellows happens. There is a music with its own distinct rhythm created; and like music, that rhythm and its key, can be regular or broken. Dylan Thomas relates that he wanted to write poetry in the beginning because he had fallen in love with words: it was the shapes and sounds of words, their music and colours, first heard from childhood, that he cared for; long before he learnt their meanings ... and this is evident in the lyric magic of the English language which pervades not only his poetry, but in like fashion, his prose. Thomas additionally, was so very, very clever in the way he often concealed his poetic devices; if one looks, it becomes evident that what on first sighting appears to be blank verse, is in fact terribly-disciplined rhyming verse ... and the rhyme itself is almost but not completely, concealed behind well-camouflaged near-rhyme.

The core energy of most creative endeavour resides in the process: the long journey itself rather than the final product: the destination. It is the strength of this involvement, irrespective of its outcomes, which drives us to create. A satisfying outcome naturally provides the fertile ground for further endeavour but it remains the medium, rather than its eventual manifestation, which ultimately provides us with the true creative impulse.

I am reminded of a discourse by Robert Graves from his 'Observations on Poetry 1922 - 1925', in which he states, "The nucleus of every poem worthy of the name is rhythmically formed in the poet's mind, during a trance-like suspension of his normal habits of thought ... learns to induce the trance in self-protection whenever he feels unable to resolve an emotional conflict by simple logic. If interrupted during this ... he will experience the disagreeable sensation of a sleep-walker disturbed; and if able to continue until the draft is completed, will presently come to himself and wonder: was the writer really he?" This is invariably what I feel ... 'Where did that come from? How did I do that? ... Did I do that?'

There remains always a sense of wonder, particularly in the wake of some very spontaneous poems, that they must have arrived from someplace outside of oneself ... a gift.

* * * * *

We now find ourselves living in this increasingly brave new age of digital evolution/revolution and with it inevitably, have come times of unprecedented diversity in practically every aspect of the arts. The cleverness of the digital tool-bag, coupled with the immediacy of communications available to one and all, has provided the means for an unbounded level of creativity in most art forms to the point where almost anyone of a mind to do so, can and does in fact, call himself or herself, artist ... and a world-class or award-winning one at that ... while the true legitimacy of such qualification is seldom, if ever, questioned. To declare is to be!

This no-holds-barred approach presents a bewildering array of choices in deciding what might or might not be regarded as art of true substance. In the minds of many, the digital tool seems to have become the end in itself: 'Never mind the quality, feel the width' ... and the true skill of the artist himself or herself often appears derived from and dependent on, the medium itself. Perhaps it matters not, whether personal skill even exists at this high-point of the consumer age, where the outward packaging continues to be more important than the contents themselves.

Inevitably, those who best take what they do, most-seriously, tend to do so apart from the mainstream and with no thought of acceptance or otherwise, by the mainstream. The truth is, this is probably how it has always been; it is just that the mainstream has now swelled to a torrent, chattering and clamouring for recognition from its vast, ether-sustained audience. The old adage, where beauty resides in the eye of the beholder, hearer or reader, seems to verify the legitimacy of 'anything-goes' more than ever before in these times of self-proclaimed greatness and mutual self-congratulation. Thankfully, there does remain an insistence and certainty for some, that there ultimately is an intangible quality which separates the gold from the dross; which elevates some expressions in every medium above most others: above the label of 'art' to that of significant, enduring Art.

In the final count, these truly-inspired creations identify themselves without the intervention of self-declaration or self-promotion but rather, by enduring in every culture, over time and circumstance: to survive the short-term lifespan of most objects in our current throw-away culture, is a goal to which many may aspire but few realise.

This remains as true for poetry as for any of the art forms; and forms abound as never before. Style-camps in poetry undoubtedly do exist, often accompanied by a spirit of elitism which tends to exclude all other forms; and yet, it is not a matter of free-verse moderns verses rhyming-verse traditionalists, or any other 'style' camps. From past to present, there are as many interpretations of what constitutes poetry as there are poets: from the 'now-moment' brevity of a Japanese haiku to the epic story-telling of a Renaissance poet, where a single poem may run to volumes composed over many years; from the ballad of a bush-poet to the accident of a 'found poem'; the legitimacy of each lies not in the selected poetic form but in the effectiveness of the poem's expression, outside of form.

A poem cannot help but be a personal expression, whether that be of one's own life, the observation of others lives, or of life and nature's many aspects; it reflects some emotional response to these things and as such, will always find a kindred soul with whom to resonate. Graffiti is also a personal expression and some could even be said to rise to the elevated level of art; most, however, remains just angry or bored defacement in the public domain. So likewise, remains the personal diatribe or shopping list randomly dissembled, no matter how much its author may declare it to be poetry. Unless it says something more, and in its manner of organisation, lifts it out of mundanity and in its telling, works real magic.

* * * * *

And on the subject of graffiti, I now have the temerity to adorn this anthology with modest examples of my own. As someone whose professional working life has been devoted to the practice of architecture, and that, primarily in the role of design architect, it is natural that I should have had some continuing interest in drawing and related pursuits.

It was an early interest with drawing in a somewhat undirected way, in my primary school years, coupled with the suggestion of a vocational guidance officer (based on one of their tests, relating to three-dimensional visualisation abilities), which led me to my initial impetus to pursue architecture as a suitable career. From that suggestion, flowed the choice of secondary school subjects, and even the choice of secondary school; amongst those subjects were technical drawing and art. Art, I enjoyed, but when I review my efforts from those years, I truly find nothing remarkable. This is probably still the case. However, I find that I have always had a modicum of natural ability which, even when neglected for years, never completely abandons me; and I do always enjoy it so much, when I rediscover it.

During my years in London, I discovered the joys of fine printmaking, specifically in the fields of serigraphy (screen-printing) and etching; with occasionally, a brief foray into mono-prints. I continued this acquaintance for some time, on my return to Australia and should have done more. Life intervened and I lost that thread for some time. Latterly, having had one dear friend in an oil painting artist for many years until his death; and more recently another, as teacher and friend until his untimely death some years ago now, also in oil painting, I have, lazily I admit, been intent on painting in oils myself ever since. Amongst these pursuits, one consistent artistic thread has run through my life: in the discipline of drawing, in various media. I enjoy drawing, be it in pencil, ink, charcoal, graphite; pen, quill, sharpened stick, bamboo pen, limp sign-writer's brush: whatever can make a mark; and if it challenges the making of a mark, so much the better.

The images selected to punctuate these pages, have been taken from various sources; mostly produced over the timeline during which, the poems were composed – not absolutely so, however. Some may find their way in from earlier times, notably during university years; nor will they necessarily serve the same space in time, that a particular poem occupies. They are certainly not intended to illustrate particular poems; simply to accompany them. The media used, likewise will vary and generally be noted with the image; a small number of images will be taken from etchings or serigraph originals in colour; in the main, they will have come from drawing media already noted. I have enjoyed their production and I trust the reader may derive some enjoyment from their inclusions in my text.

Brad Drew

12th October 2015

(Emended 10th April 2020)

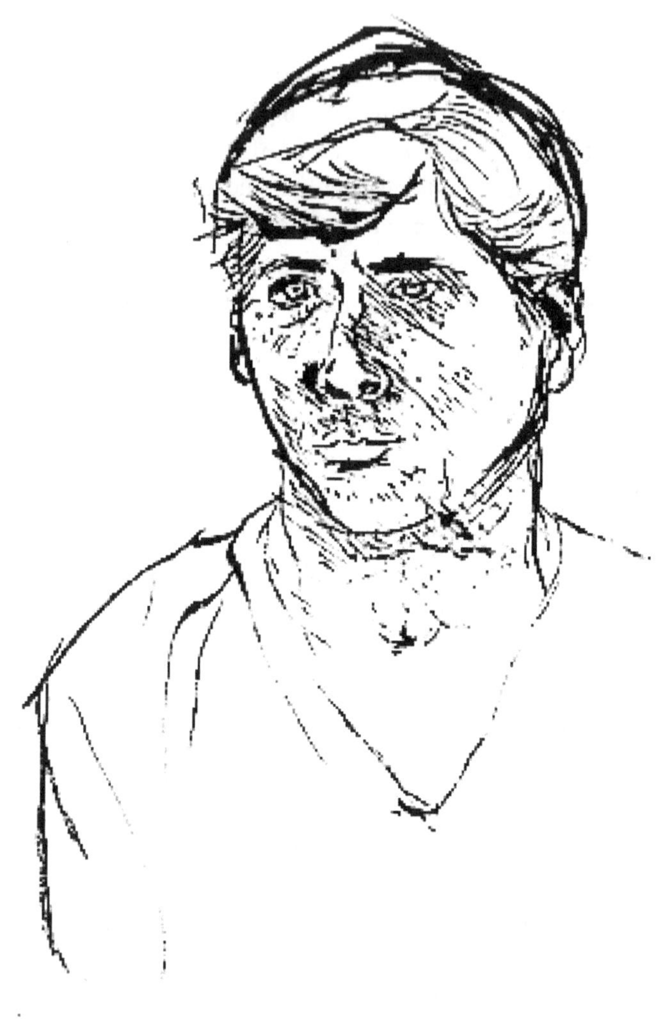

'SELF PORTRAIT'
Quill liner & Indian ink on Fabriano Paper, 1983

CONTENTS

PREFACE TO THE REVISED
EDITION:
FOREWARD BY BRUCE DAWE AO
INTRODUCTION:

THE POEMS:

BRISBANE 1973 :

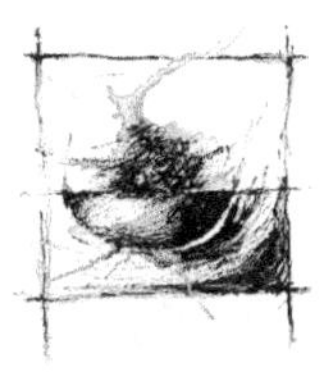

LONDON 1974 TO 1977 :

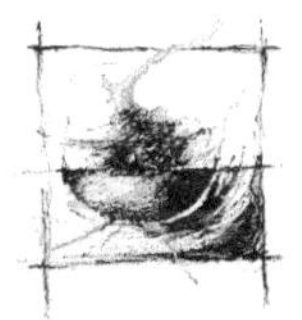

POST-LONDON:
BRISBANE MAY 2001 TO JUNE 2003 :

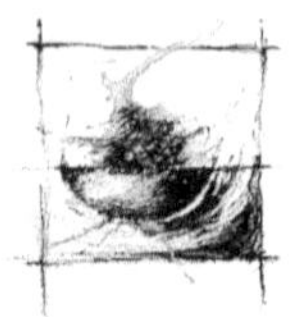

BLACKALL RANGE
JULY 2003 TO NOVEMBER 2015 :

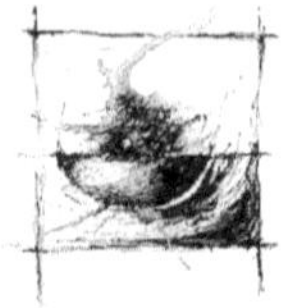

BLACKALL RANGE LATER POEMS
DECEMBER 2015 TO MAY 2020 :

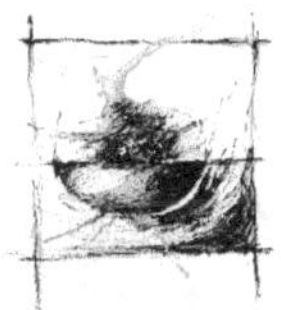

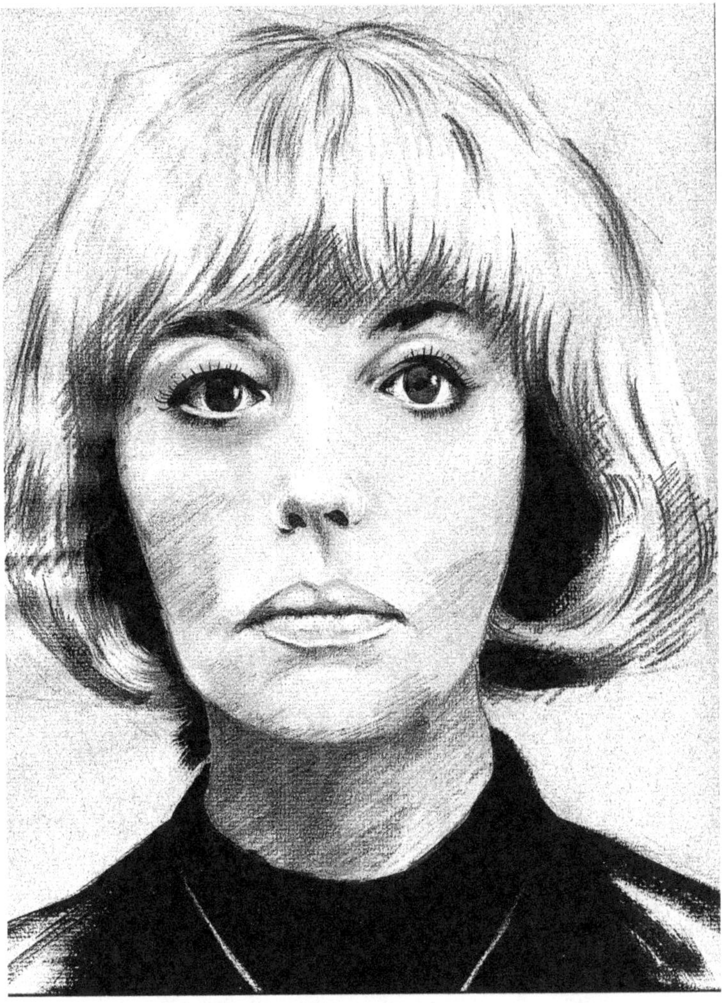

'JEAN MOREAU'
Pencil & mixed media on Ingres Paper, 1976

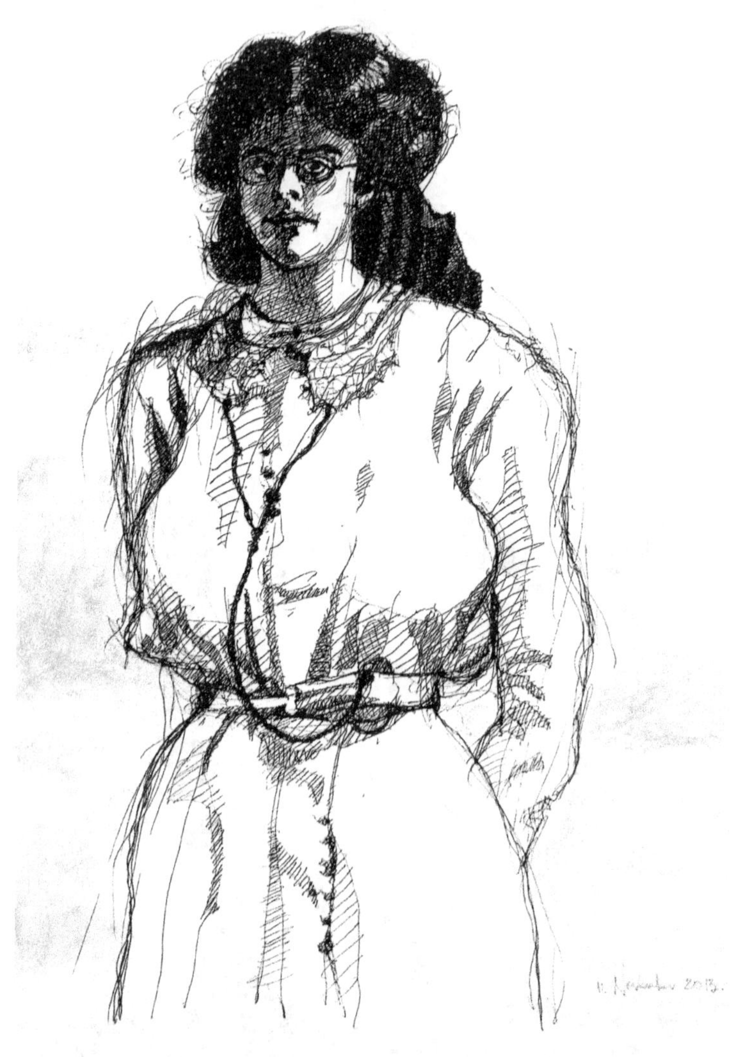

'A NURSING FRIEND OF MY GRANDFATHER, c. 1916'
Rollerball & charcoal on Cartridge Paper, 2016

BRISBANE 1973

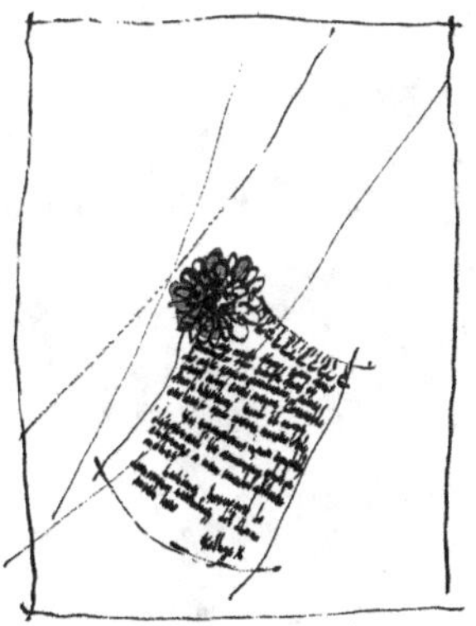

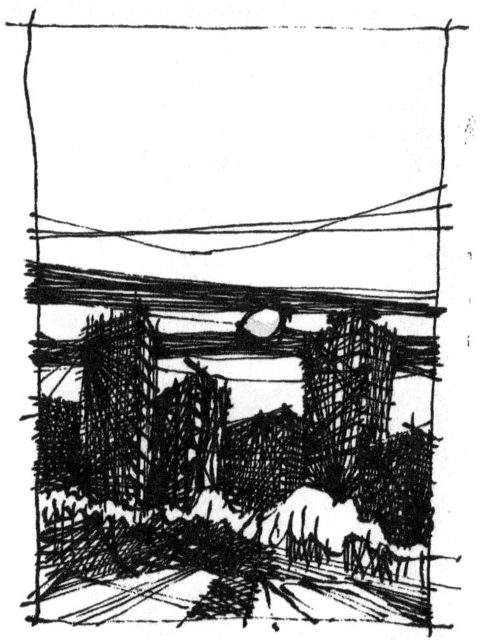

'CITY LIGHTS & GIBBOUS MOONS'
Graphos pen with Indian ink on Ingres Paper, 1973

EVENING

Quiet now ... city lights glitter
a barge moves slowly upstream
factory lights fall on deaf waters
while cars move by: an endless stream
to pause at traffic lights outside my window.
A lone breeze stirs
barely moving trees outside
nor the light above my table.
Perhaps tomorrow will be cooler ...

The days move slowly
the nights so fast
impatient to feel the dawn.
Night carries oneness pervading
bringing the start of new day –
peace, and excitement, and cool.
The days exert controls
as nights offer freedoms, and love ...
companionships to enjoy:
music, theatre, dinners
fresh air, darkness, lights and bed.
Another world and life.

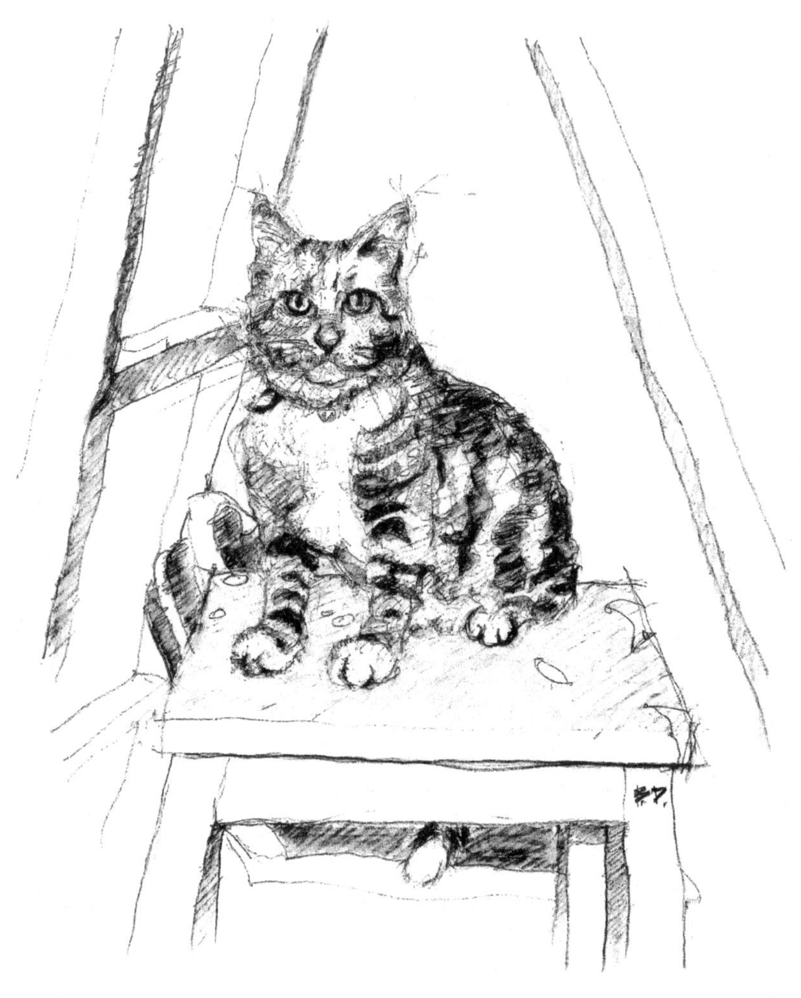

'DENYA'

Aquarelle graphite pencil & wash on Cartridge Paper, 2018

TWELVE HOURS LATER

Fans spinning
Breeze stirring
Traffic bustling
Heat creeping ...
The seconds drag around the clock-face
While March seems so very far away.
Last night, you seemed quite distant
Or was that mere imagination?

TOP TIGGER

I wish I had seen
Or even been, your cat ...
Black, with a white bow tie,
One white spat
(second on the right)
And big green eyes.

THE WISE AMONG US

The wise among us shun love,
Green fields and distant skies.
The wise will live and breathe each day
As the cow chews endless cud ...
Their ways are simple and direct,
Their lives tick steadily by the clock
Toward the same, inevitable end.
But then, the wise have never loved.

I HAVE LOOKED

I have looked for you
in faces passing on the street.
I have listened for your footfall
in the corridors of life
and waited for its pause outside my door.
I have watched you
and smelt your smell
to absorb each precious moment
of our times which seem so short.
I take in every detail of you,
wishing for no need to recourse memory
while every moment of life with you is now.

YESTERDAY

Across the Arctic plains
down slopes toward the sea,
words and thoughts can often rush
like Lemmings, bent
on mindless self-destruction.

Their drive, they never comprehend
nor pause to contemplate ...
blizzard-like, the driven thoughts
and words pass over, rushing
for the cliff-edge in their haste.

In wintering haste, the chilling blast,
so borne of sensitivity and rustlings
in the shifting breeze of self,
will drop some leaves,
then ebb away, to quietly subside.

Understanding holds the buds
left in their wake,
awaiting spring's emergence
from chill winter's short embrace,
to flourish, on each empty branch once more.

AT MY WINDOW

Gibbous moons rise
full and yellow –
on occasion, red ...
when dust is in the air.
So too, do full moons,
new moons, half moons
like tonight's.
Were I a fisherman of the stars,
I would snare one in a net of dreams
to lay it at your door.

Lightning, when it storms
(so you tell me)
spreads in wondrous sheets
across its bed, or falls
in deadly chains to plunge and strike,
causing you concern.
Were I a blacksmith in the clouds,
I would collect them up
to fashion in my forge, bright necklaces of light
to place around your neck.

IF ONLY

If only you would come as once you did
when love was fresh and came unburdened;
to enter in by the midnight silence,
sharing your warmth ...
And whispered invitations to fly
from the midst of evenings owned by others.
Mornings of waking to the dawn,
making mad dashes through her early light,
returning you to your still-sleeping household.

Insane dashes back from the distant coast
along an empty highway; while I,
striving to drive and you, driving me
as if the car had a mind of its own.
Partings that consumed hours
and meetings that knew no limits ...
storms and moons and dinners.
If only you would come as once you did.

NUN.895

I watch for red volkswagons
outside my flat ...
I watch for red volkswagons
and listen for them at my door,
ever hoping that you'll come
or be, in fact, already here.

Entering, I look about for signs
of your sometimes earlier presence.
No notes here now, but oftentimes
in clues ... damp washer
or a toothbrush left unsheathed ...
your clothes, or records played.

Knowing that you've been,
I listen for red volkswagons ...
and full of hope, I watch.

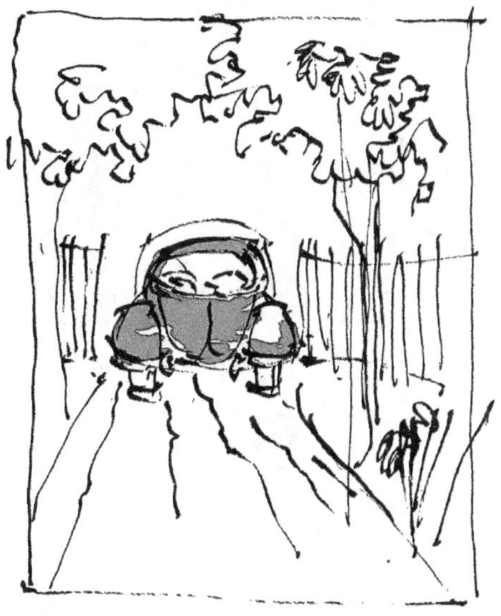

'RED VOLKSWAGONS OUTSIDE MY FLAT'
Graphos pen with Indian ink on Ingres Paper, 1973

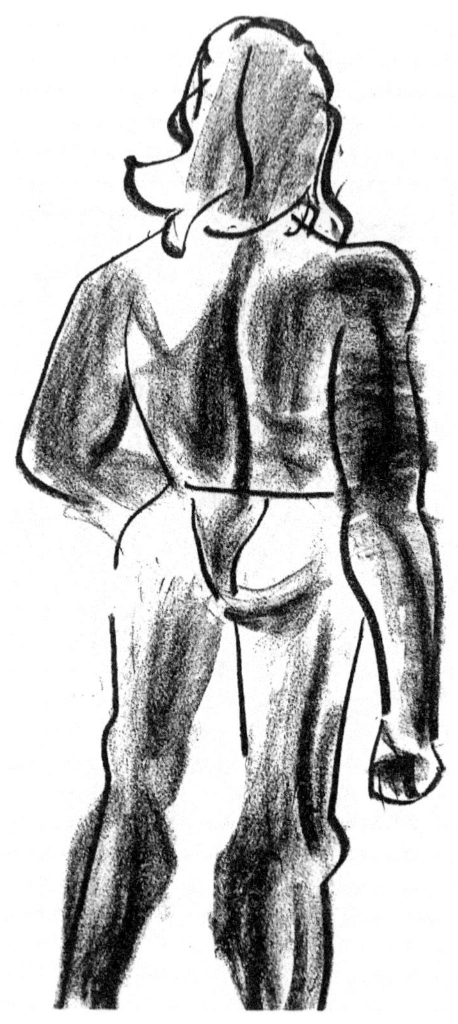

'NORMAN'

Compressed charcoal on Newsprint, 1966

LONDON:
April 1974 to June 1977

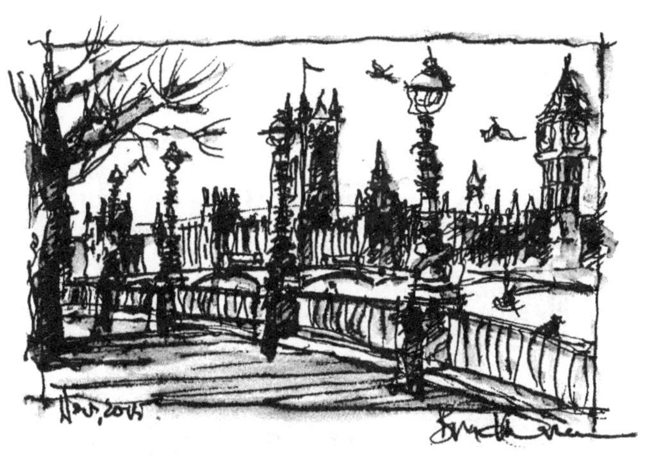

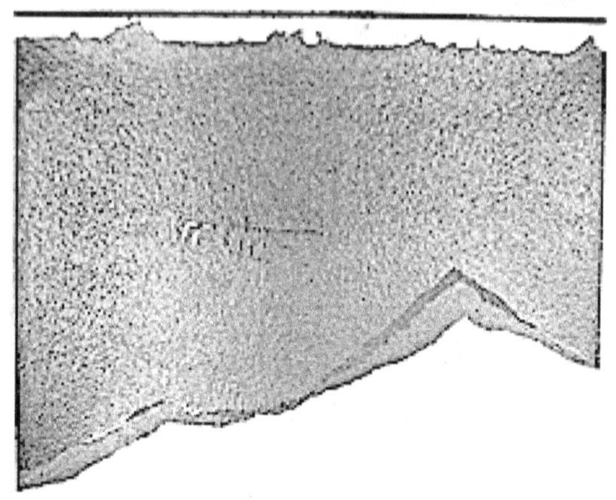

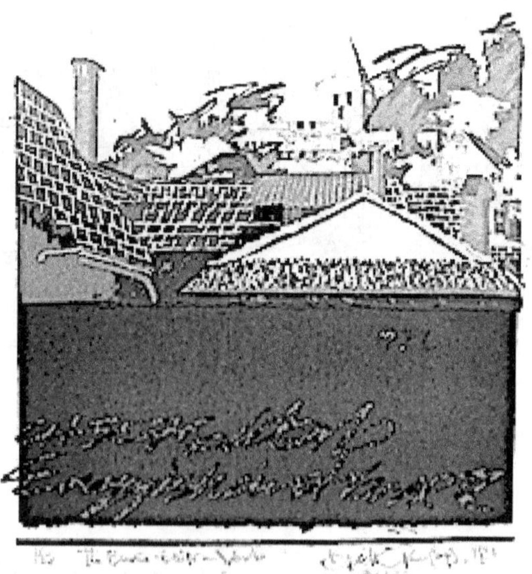

'THE BERNE SUITE – WORB'

Screenprint on Arches Dessin Paper,1981

(From the full-colour original)

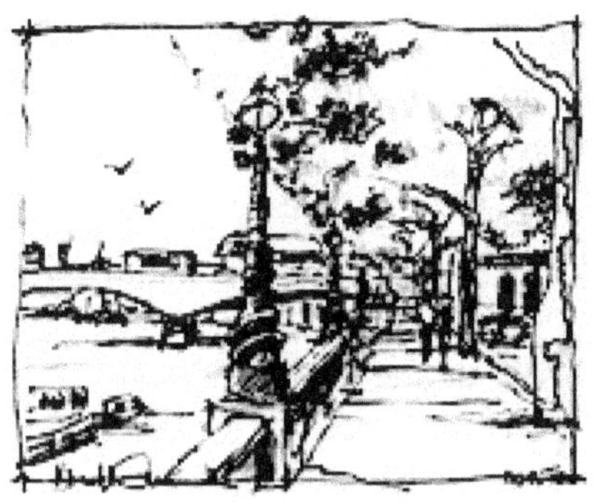

'THE EMBANKMENT'

Rollerball & wash on Arches Paper, 2015

SOUTHBANK BLUES: For Bernard

I had a friend here once, who loved a girl too well –
but never really should have done:
because one fine day, she went straight out
to marry someone else.

These facts established, we went to a concert;
listened to some dancers who,
periodically would slip on a large banana,
written thoughtfully by the show's SM,
like the keystone of a silent movie,
on centre-stage, stage-left –
for all customers' enjoyments:
in lieu of winter's frozen pools,
for fools, on busy pavements.

Intermission and the twenty minute
Southbank bar-rush, with
beers, martinis, plastic cups ...
and ruminated both, on loves
who might have been;
had been, but weren't –
and watched a surging sea of girls
with pretty breasts, pert asses
who flowed around us like an adolescent dream;
and started then at faces –
not quite faces we had known.

Much later, as we
walked above the rivered lights,
back home for The Embankment,
we declined to take a final drink,
because it was a long Tube home ...
and suddenly grown cold.

PUTNEY BRIDGE

I loved you –
Oh! So well ... that summer –
and tonight a girl stood by me,
on Putney Bridge in rain,
waiting for the bus and looking
so very much, like you.
I almost answered to her eye –
only, she may not have been you;
and of that, I was afraid.

I stood there with your phantom,
in two years' of distant rain
and that last of summer's
dimming traffic glow ...
to let first one bus, then another,
go lumbering on their ways;
waiting to mull upon your memory,
just a little further.

And I sit here still ...
on this steaming, empty bus
in this empty London night,
while tears of rain
sweep moist-lidded windows;
weep monsoons of memories,
of one far-distant summer's night –
abandoned to the damp embrace
of a steamy bus and the hissing kiss
of slick wet tires ...
while Cloverdale Park Nursery,
seems so very far away.

POSTSCRIPT:

Remembering
how something never was ...
Searching
where something never is ...
Half-day removed –
still there
and starting at visions
in rain-spattered streets.

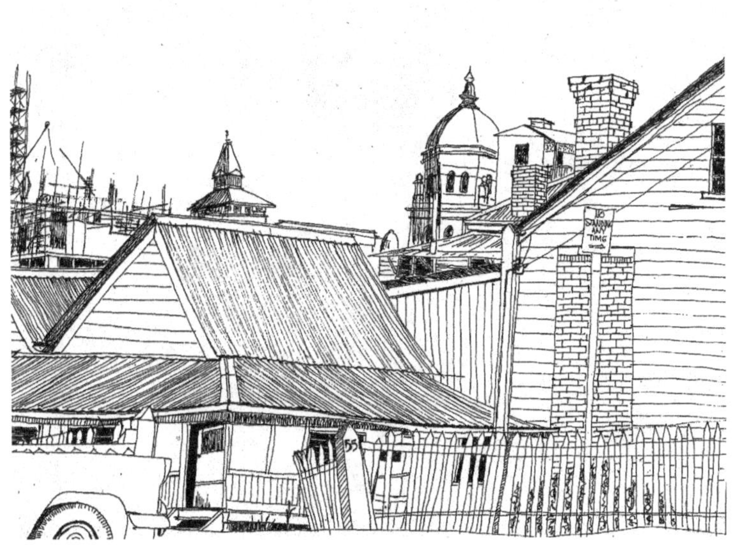

'SPRING HILL STREET'
Rapidograph on Cartridge Paper, 1966

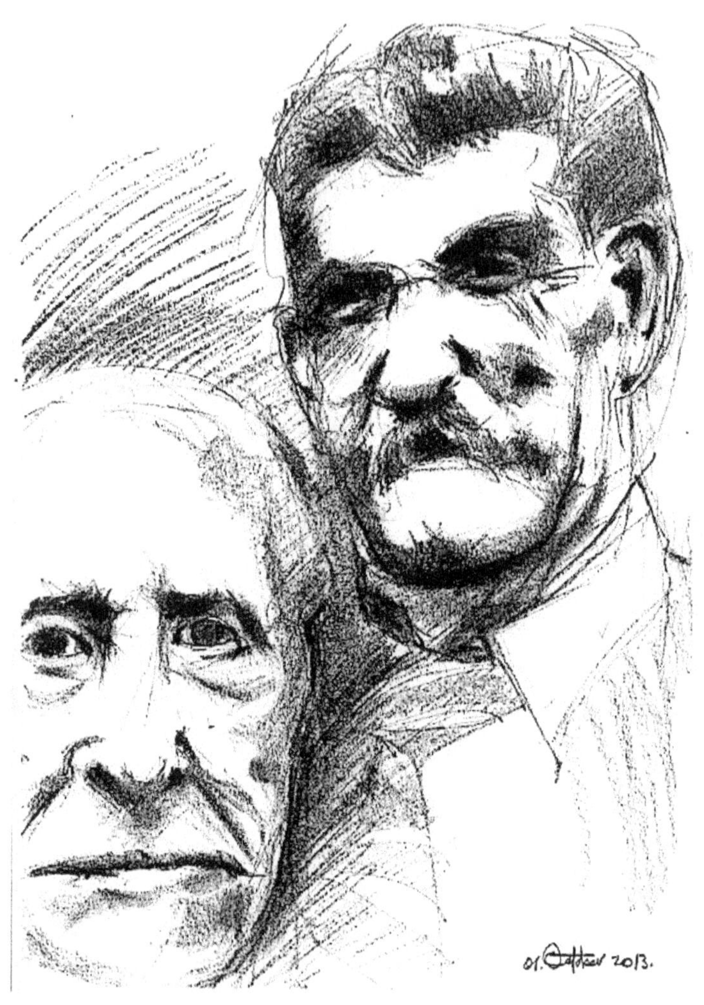

'MY GREAT GRANDPARENTS:
ROBERT & ELIZABETH HIGGENSON' :
Graphite block on Cartridge Paper, 2013

NEW YEAR 1975

I sit alone tonight, waiting ...
waiting in solemn ceremony ...
waiting to take nineteen-seventy-five down
from its cardboard, top-of-cupboard prison –
waiting for the day of its parole,
these past two months.

I sit alone tonight, waiting ...
waiting for someone to come and say,
'Hey! It's New Year's
and you sit here all alone,
waiting to let that silly box down off the shelf,
down to let next year run loose?
Come out and have a drink!'
Only ... there's no one coming.

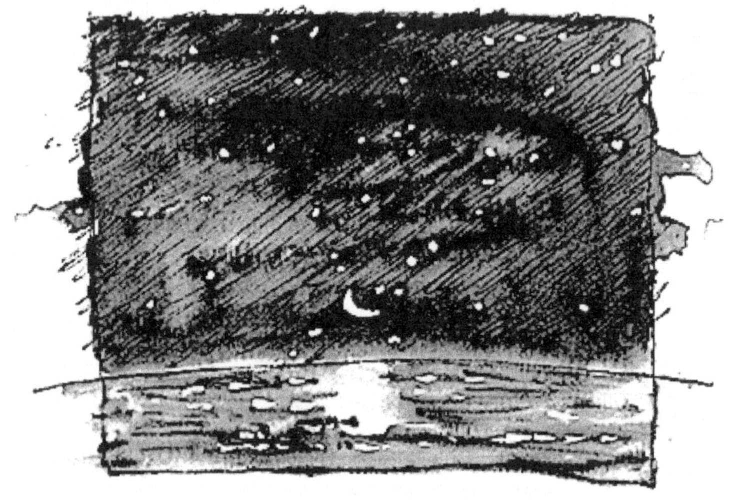

'LONGING, SEEN IN PRE-DAWN PORTENTS'
Rollerball & wash on Arches Paper, 2006

PROCESSION

Processions of days rush by
in endless sweeps of beating
prehistoric wings, fabricated
from shards of long-stored memories ...
mementos of progression and reprise.

It's March again and soon comes spring –
smiles and flattering attentions reign
and everything is beautiful again.

SYLVIE

At least it's a luck
you don't close your windows –
it's not more than two hours,
I would have had to wait
behind a door!
I go home and come back
with your salad at around eight!

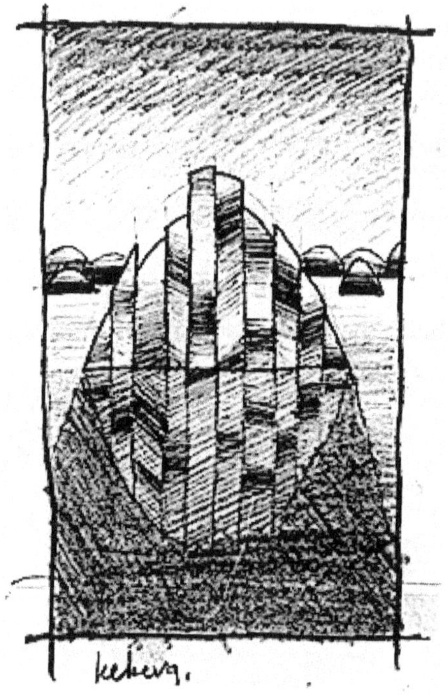

Notebook pencil study for 'ICEBERG' screenprint : 1979

DAWN HAIKU

Amber-crisp dawning:
Dragonfly passes on sails
Gossamer-woven.

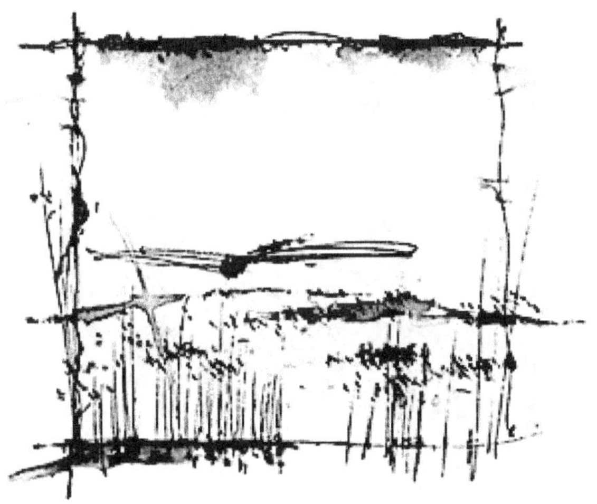

'DRAGONFLY'
Rollerball & wash on Arches Paper, 2007

STREET HAIKU

Shaven heads, painted;
Finger-slapping brazen discs;
Handing out incense.

SPRING TANKA

Golden-skinned lovers,
Garlanded with beads of light,
Licking dawn's warm breath
On moistly-sweet tongues of night –
These perfect first daffodils.

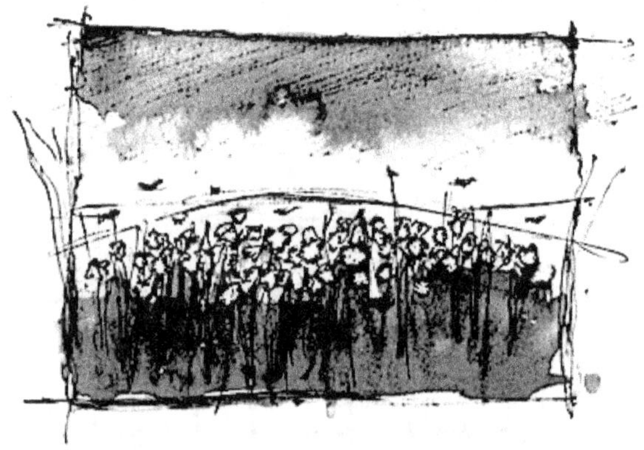

'DAFFODILS'
Rollerball & wash on Arches Paper, 2007

SUNDAY TANKA

How gently there hangs
And quietly drops, the soft
Of this spring twilight –
Mingling and lost in your eyes,
Touched by the warmth of your smile.

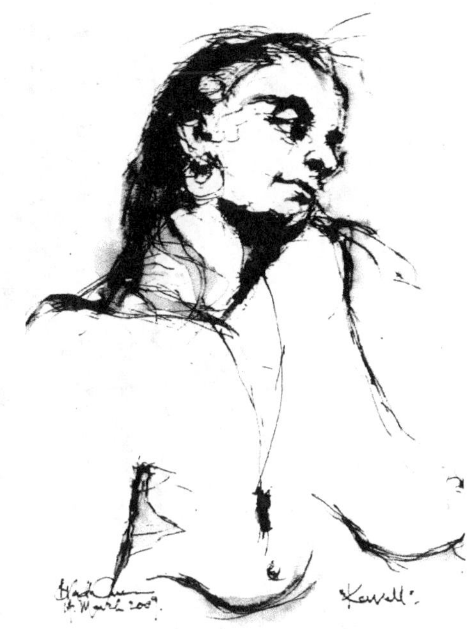

'HEAD OF A GIRL'
Rollerball on Arches Paper, 2007

THE COACHMAN

Timeless dusk
and faceless breath of vast intrigue
who guide with easy hand, this coach:
take me –
willing guest and passenger of endless dawn
I'll ride beside your presence
trusting and keeping
the smells of each new sunrise that you bring.

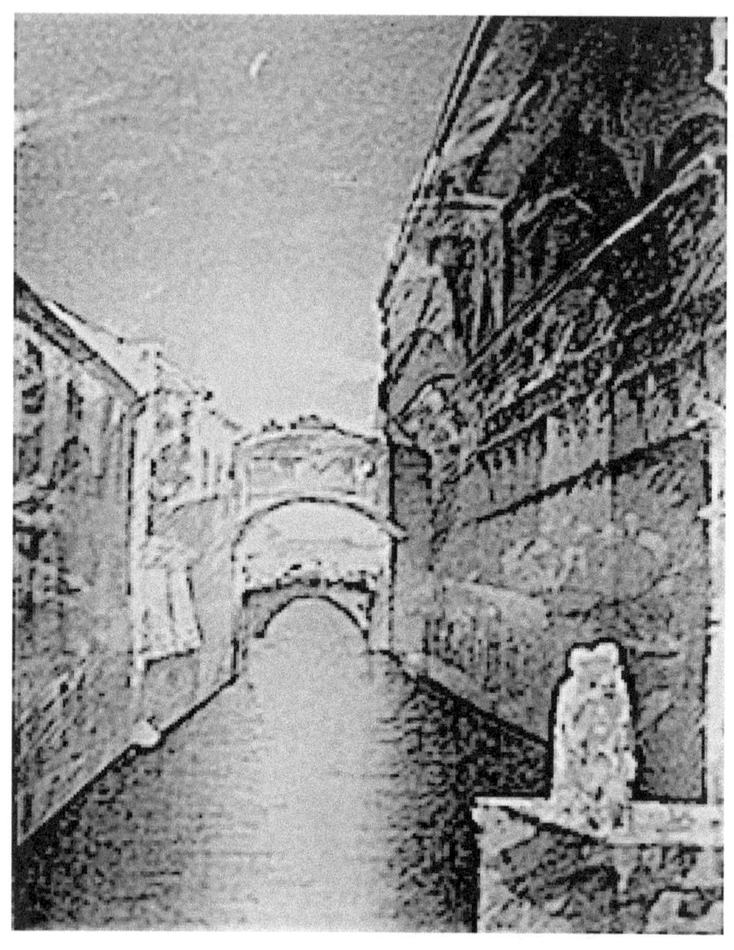

'BRIDGE OF SIGHS, VENICE'
Screenprint on Arches Dessin Paper, 1983
(From the full-colour original)

PASTORALE

Nestled by your side,
I watched you sleeping –
And fields of poppies
Broke across your cheeks;
Your smile rose up
And, draped with pearls,
Stepped out to dance among them.

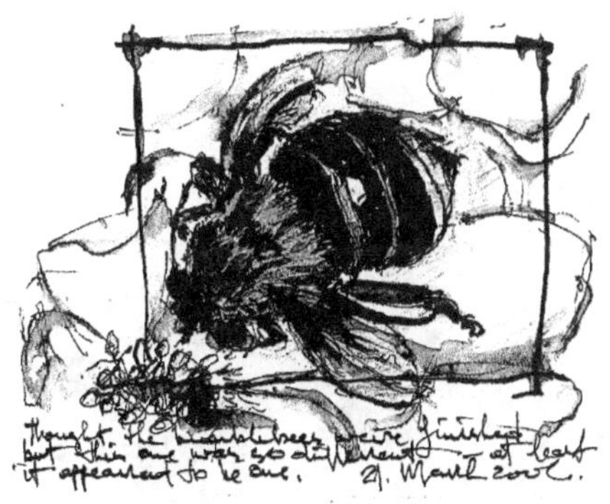

'BUMBLEBEE'
Rollerball & wash on Arches Paper, 2006

TANKA ON YOUR DEPARTURE

What might be written,
When the sun has extinguished
And dimmed this fresh world?
Wait! It is only eclipsed –
Behind the moon, it burns still.

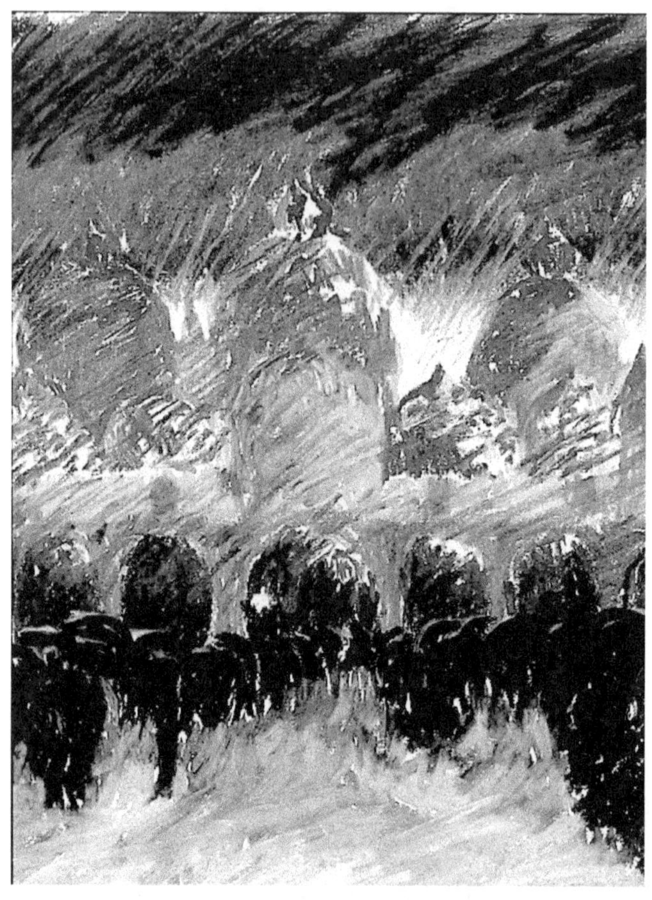

Study for 'ST MARK'S SQUARE' Screenprint
Pastel on Cartridge Paper, 1981
(From the full-colour original)

YOU HAVE NOT CHANGED

You have not changed ...
And winds that bore you from me
on sails of neon men-of-war, full-thrust
past tides of cities, lit with efflorescent beads
of dew in time-shined spores;
have kept you ... I, the wind-maker.

You have not changed ...
And I, the firefly and moth of constant dreams
and shifting sands: these fluxing tides surging
in the glow of ancient keeps
built high on wave-strewn coastlines;
have kept you ... I, the wind-maker.

You have not changed ...
And clouds that bore you in me light as dusk
on distant slopes of stream-swept jade
to glide on shining sleds of glass
fresh-honed from Chartres' ancient rose;
have kept you ... I, the born-on-wind.

You have not changed –
And youthful blooms in forest depths
light with their fires, the phoenix keep
fanned high by winds that bore you to me;
sails that kept you ... You, the wind-rider.

WAKING POEM

Seven a.m. – and a jet just swam
across my morning sunbath,
wiping its shadow over my face:
a washer-full of last week's words,
scribbled on a subway wall.

GUINEVERE'S TANKA

Cassidy's is the
World's first, patented timelock:
Braving tall seas on
Sails, fashioned from the plankton
Of Camelot's silent sighs.

'

DO NOT FEAR

Do not fear for
the sweet, sibilant whispers
of the rustling leaves of sorrow ...
For sighing sings the softest
of the sibyl's songs.

POEM FOR RON

Another morning at the office
as he sits behind me, marching on that apple –
advancing over it:
like treading the forgotten bones
of a long-lost general, at dawn,
on plains of ancient Babylon.

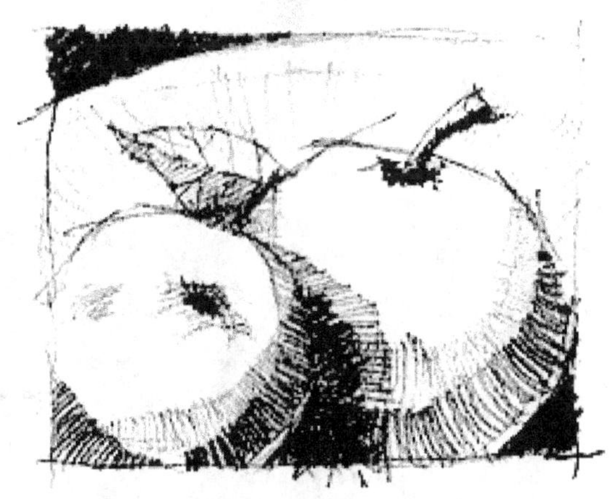

'APPLES'
Pencil on Arches Paper, 2006

HOLLOW HAIKU

Springtime love affairs
Should claim only the stout heart –
It's summer again.

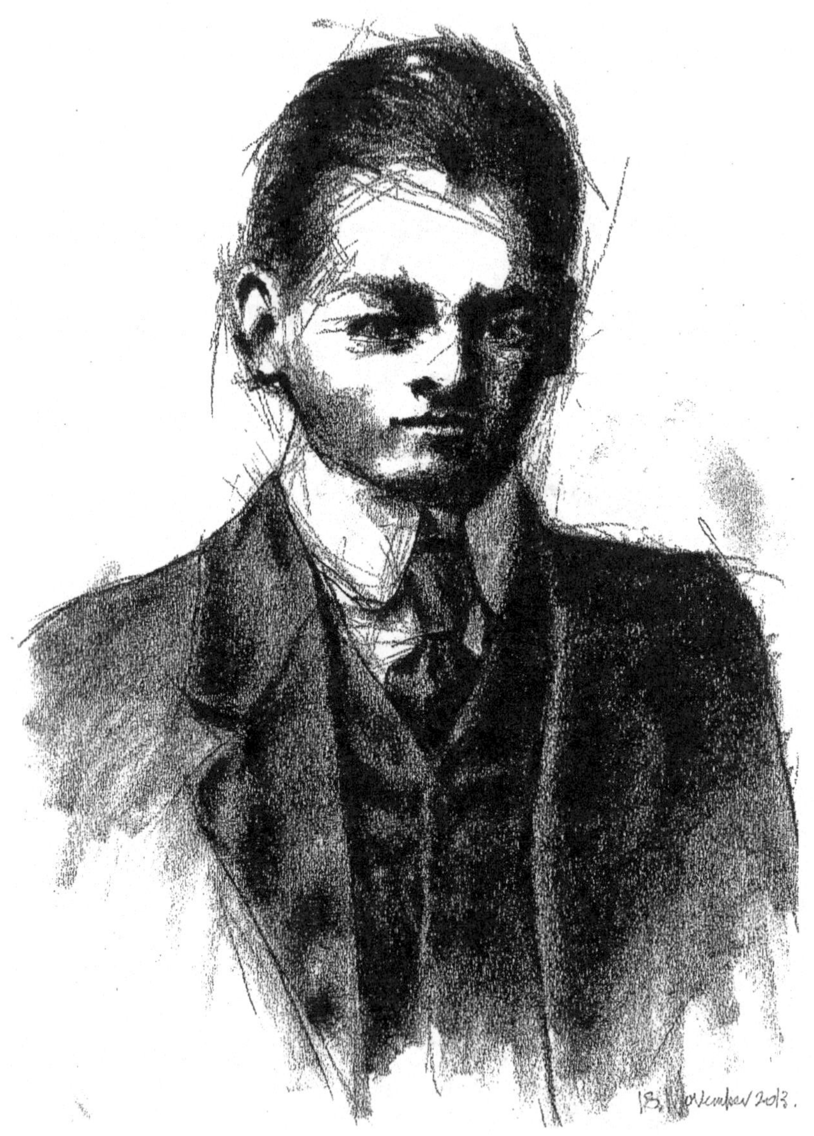

'A FRIEND OF MY GRANDFATHER, FROM WW1'
Conte crayon on Cartridge Paper, 2013

THE KEEPER

The keeper is lost –
And losing, so the unsheathed ring:
Time's annulary, bared in solemn gambit,
Gambled for an unseen queen –
She rings the pealing
Of the hours and houri, measured out upon
The bane Achilles held –
She keeps, and holding,
Holds his unkeeped heart
And bares it to the light of day.

The keeper is lost –
And keeping, keeps his solaced keep:
Kept high on castled crags, between the distance
Of his bursting soul's intent –
In his watch-housed sleep,
He's marked her measures;
Timed her hours of queen-shod waking –
For the outlawed swain, Astarte weep:
For he's pawned his heart
And bears it from the light of day.

(Written originally in London 1975 and, as fate would have it,
a prologue to 'The Fisher Swain', some twenty-five years,
and half a world later, in Brisbane.)

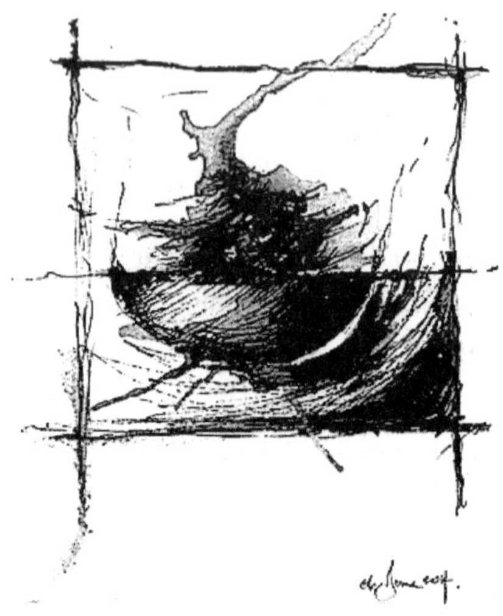

'GRAIL STUDY"
Rollerball & wash on Arches Paper, 2014

LONDON SPRING

The lissom curving of your spine
reminds me of antelopes
in a sun-swept day ...
So, often-times, I walk behind you.

IN MY ASYLUM

You see, I have this crazy impulse
to follow every woman
who looks vaguely like you.
You could be leading me home.

There, every taxi's door
sounds like your footstep.
Consequently, I make a lot of false starts ...
like a blind sprinter on an empty track.

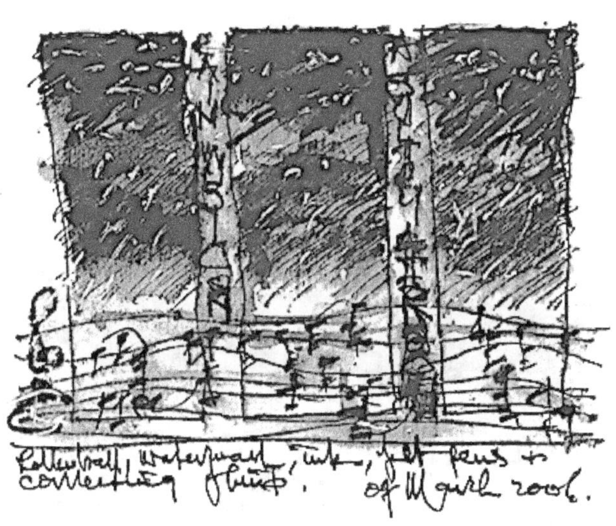

'RAIN MUSIC'
Rollerball, wash & correction pen on Arches Paper, 2006

COLUMBUS

I played in the bath
With your rubber duck, last night ...
Pretending you were there
With chrome-plate wings,
Waiting to return it, like Columbus
Sailing from the New World,
Under fair skies and
The gentle hint of dusk,
Between the valley of your thighs.

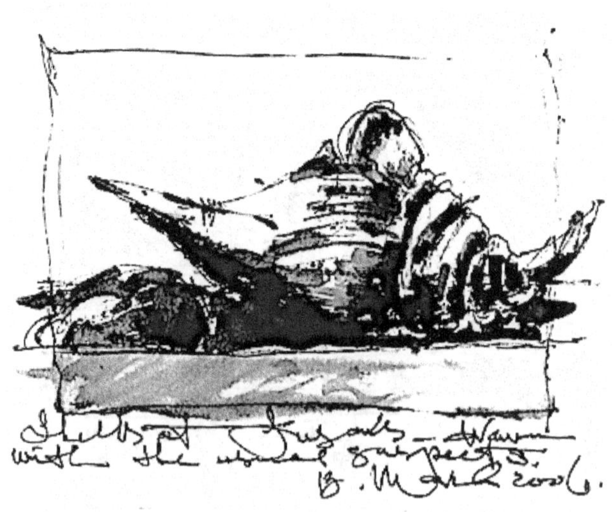

'SHELLS' :
Rollerball & wash on Arches Paper, 2006

REAP THE MARCH WINDS

Reap the March winds
for a few days' madness.
Steal the dead of night
from the Blind King's purse
and, singing in the madhouse heat,
reach out ...
for she'll never come this way again.

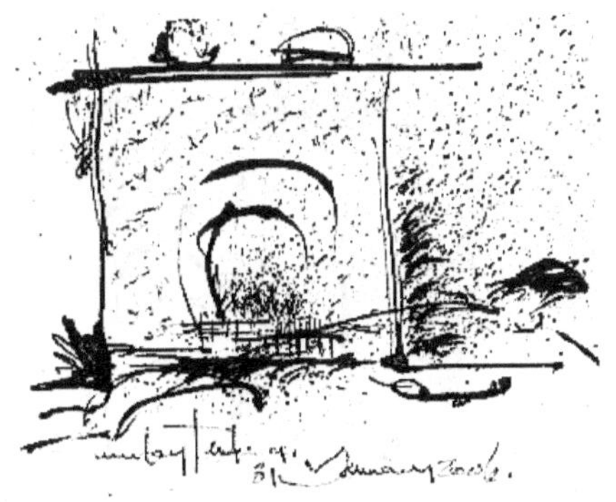

'GORDON PLACE FIREPLACE'
Quill & Ink on Arches Paper, 2007

WAKING POEM 2

Night's ghost flees misted window panes,
fire glowing; growing in the grate.
Lone shaft of wintered sunlight
strokes the window jamb
and falteringly,
feels its way across the room.

SUNDAY TUBE TO PUTNEY BRIDGE

My hands are shaking today
Because I've had too much coffee
And not enough black sleep ...
Or, was it coming to see you?

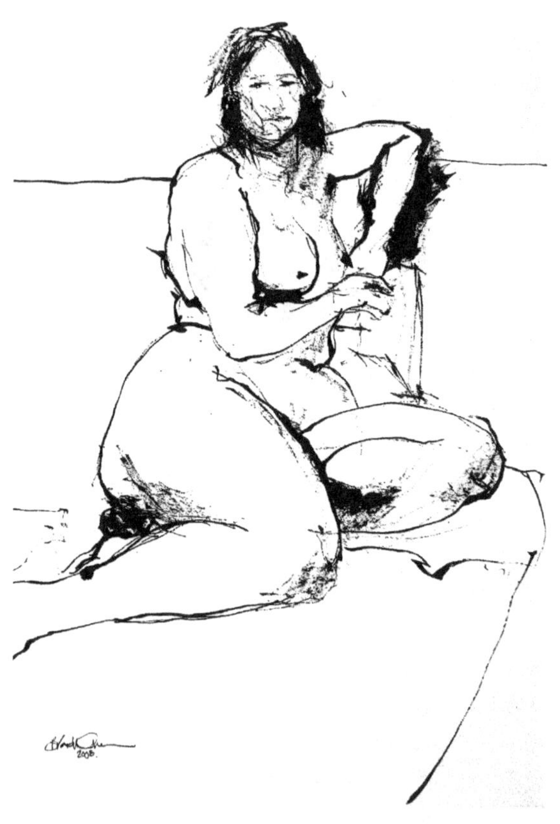

'SEATED WOMAN'
Sharpened stick with Indian ink on Cartridge Paper, 2009

NONE OTHER ...

You walked my way ...
and drew warm vapours of scented fields
across my sight.
You rose to greet me ...
and in so doing, loosed one thousand
shimmering jewels from your lips.

You brought this day, deep in your pocket
to show only me in the stillness of night.

You stirred in my world ...
and the hint of your movement
sent rainbow-blessed insects
from flickering leaves, rising
and soaring to welcome your light.

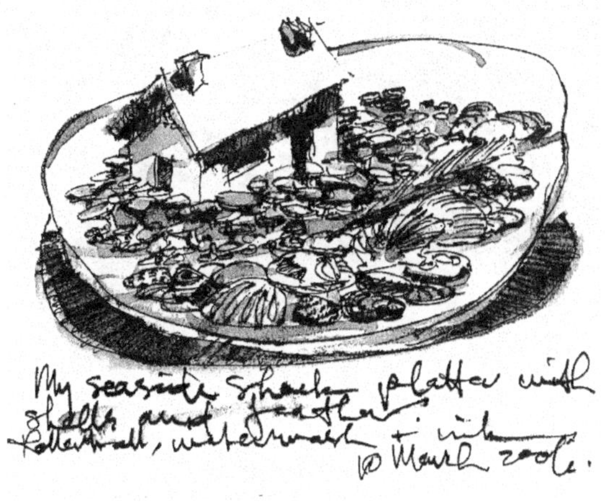

'SEASIDE PLATTER'
Rollerball & wash on Arches Paper, 2006

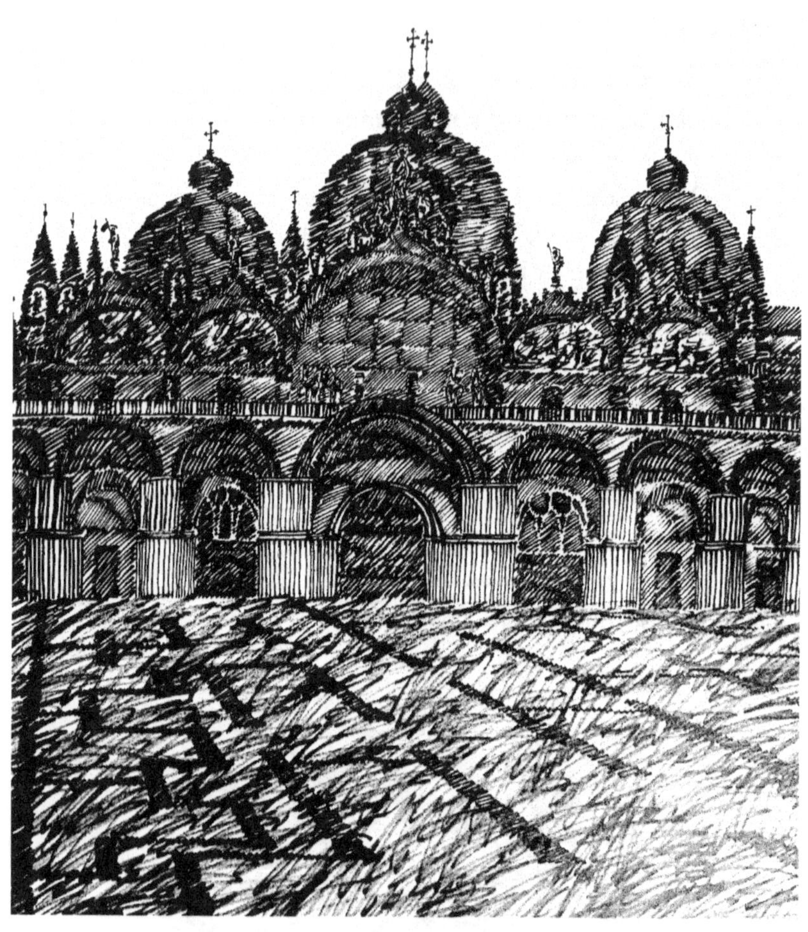

'ST MARK'S, VENICE'
Opaque felt marker on Tracing Paper, 1981
Stencil master for screenprint

'

TRAIN:
EIGHT-THIRTY PADDINGTON
TO PLYMOUTH

Eight-thirty train to Exeter ...
Two hours and forty minutes:
Reading-Taunton-Exeter St Davids –
    What's Plymouth?

England slipping by in nameless haze
As the Inter-City knife-slice pulses ::
Throbs :: and penetrates :: in lengthy intercourse
On rolling Devon fields ...
And holdings, cottages and barns,
Hedgerows, fences, stiles and downs ...
Struggling greenery trying hard –
    These waterways and trees.

Pulsing :: Throbbing ::
Coursing down the thighs of Noble England.
Grey ... grey blankets draped,
Draped in loose soiled folds caressing,
Clinging these recumbent loins ...
Ecstasy of the Eight-thirty
    Paddington-to-Plymouth.

Second lunge-thrust of the day,
Slipping smoothly down, day-long ...
Coming :: Coming :: Oh! I'm coming!
... Rape of England!
'LIBS THROW A SPANNER',
Read the headlines ...
On Her back and I'm here, languishing
     In Inter-City come.

Black-faced sheep, cottages
And rolling fields, forever.
... Ah! ... A junkyard!
Scrapped and beat-up, dented,
Battered, rusted, rotting cars:
How quaint! Where's spring?
     And where are you, my Love?

Trees burning ... burning-out
On sheltered side of hill
And Mother's home
With children playing at her knees –
Tends the kitchen,
Keeps the home fires burning
While Father's burning tree stumps
     On the hill.

Embers glow in mist-swathed morning;
Lunch approaching,
Father's coming, all is well ...
     And England lives.

Spring coming :: Blankets hugging ::
British Rail's swollen member throbs;
Throbs on through the South-West,
Under blankets, dirtied
With its countless comes.
... Wasn't it good, My Love? My Loves?
You, whom I loved, and love;
I bear you with me, as we make it ::
Sigh and make it :: Sigh and brake it ::
     Braking it :: In Taunton ::

Spread-out under milky skies,
Stretched from star to star,
There :: Here :: We were frozen ::
There :: forever ::
In moments :: that were ::
Before they :: That are ...
And I am locked here :: now ::
     As I have been :: Will be ...

Thudding :: Pounding :: Throbbing ::
Pulsing :: Post-Taunton Blues ...
Oh God! I'm coming!
Tadpole legionnaire, I've closed the ranks.
St David's discharge and I'm gone:
Just another spunky frog,
Lost-in-action ... Exeter,
Thirty-first day of March,
     Nineteen Seventy-seven.

(Written during the course of a morning rail journey
from London to Exeter: a regular event
on office business – having recently read
Allen Ginsberg's lengthy poem,'Iron Horse' ...
an act, inspired by, rather than emulating, that work.)

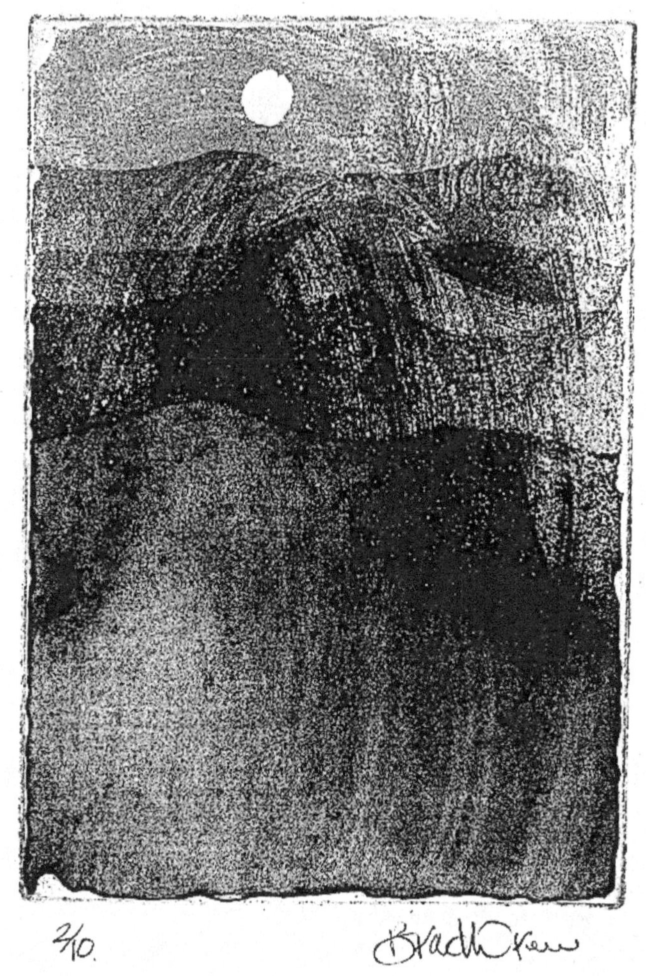

'LANDSCAPE WITH DEVON HILLS'
Zinc plate etching on rag paper, 1976

POST-LONDON: BRISBANE
MAY 2001 TO JUNE 2003

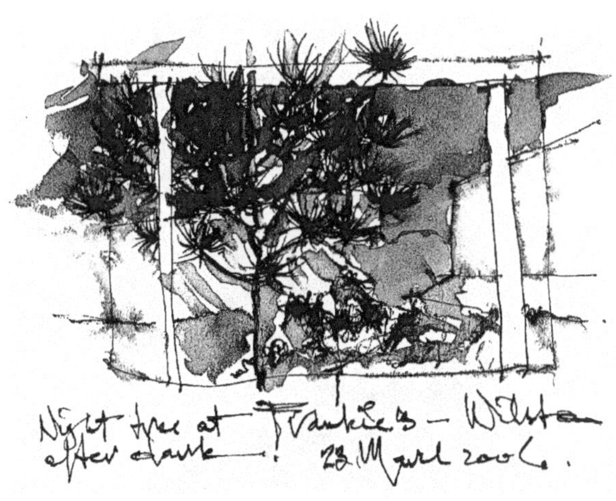

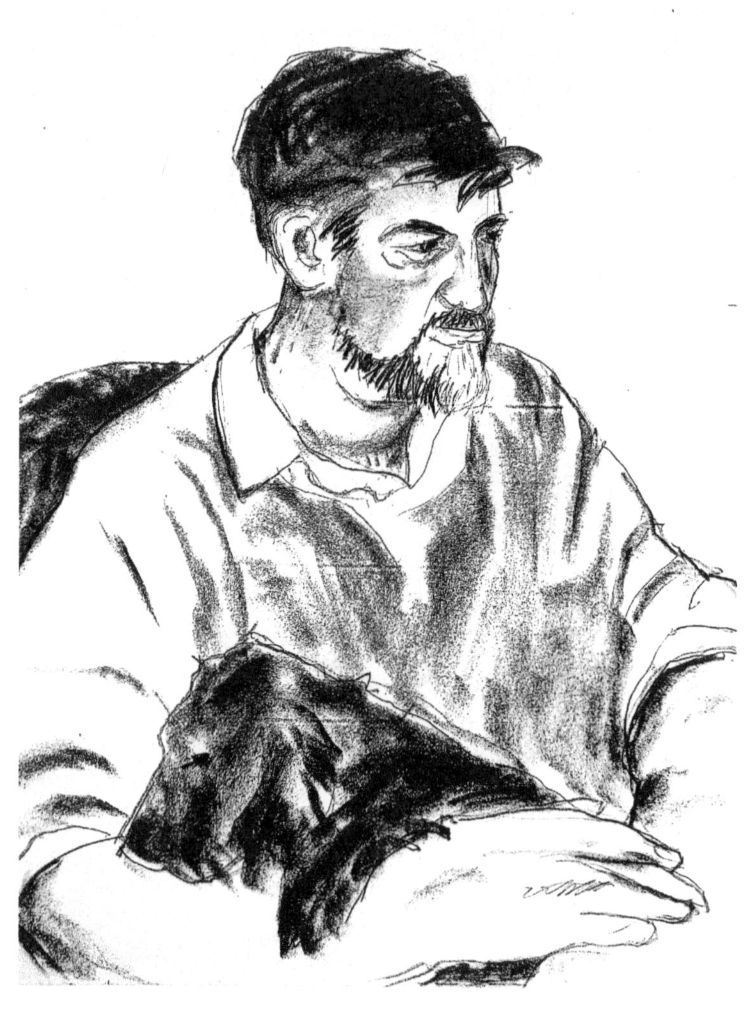

'FRANK & LILLY'
Compressed charcoal on Newsprint, 2002

THE FISHER SWAIN

Exiled heart and outlawed swain.
Each night: a year – he dreamt in vain;
dreamt of longing and desire –
each night: a year;
each day: a fire.
Seven, and-one-half millennia
thus, he dreamt ... the Keeper-lost:
so great the cost
of unseen queen and all she meant ...
and so, he dreamt.
　　Astarte wept –

For his pawned heart, wept
and weeping, hid it from the light of day.
Distanced, bursting soul's intent ...
the queen-shod, nightly pealing rent
one heart in two;
kept one half and all its healing.
Bell-keeper and Time's broker:
bearer of Fate's annulary,
bared in silence long ago ...
solemn gambit, unseen queen.
　　Astarte wept –

Whose the tolling; whom the weeping;
whose the dreaming; whom the sleeping?
Distanced in his bursting soul, he slept
and dreamt ... and dreaming, dreamt
of being lost and all it cost.
　　Sleeping thus, he dreamt again –

Hours and houri lost to sight,
years sweep by in endless flight;
the beat of wings drown out his plight.
Their beating lulls his sleep at night,
quells his dreams, his quest for life.
To still the throngs who storm his gates
Penelope-like, he undertakes
to knit a shawl, a home, a cairn ...
and knitting thus, some gesture make,
to quench this thirst which will not slake.
    And once, he dreamt –

Waking, dreamt he saw her yet;
knew that he could not forget
her face, her form, her inner light ...
her sight and sound, that burned so bright ...
and burning,
put his soul to flight,
forever owning all his nights.
    Astarte slept –

Sleeping thus, his heart she kept.
Of purpose lost, of fire bereft,
he put away his joys and slept;
wounded with a toxin deep,
he sought some solace in his sleep.
Queen-shod pealing in the night;
grail-quest fire that burned so bright ...
wound complete, he saw her yet.
Wondered then, would she forget
one brief, one flaring light.
    Astarte slept –

Eternity, he dreams and sleeps ...
sweet sleep: an opiate to his days.
He knits his shawl and seeks a way
to find some meaning to his fate;
the wound he would, if could, negate.
Another place, he saw the gleam;
tried to forget what might have been ...
to put away, both soul and mind
believing that, with friends and time:
distractions of another kind,
    his wound would heal and slowly bind.

The world he sought, whilst mostly good,
had not the test of time withstood ...
    the rigours of a heart bereft.

The friends he gained, pained for his plight
and heard his emptiness at night ...
besieged by calls of night-shod queen,
core of whom he once had been:
the span of which, however slight,
he'd been her passion for one night
    or two, or three, or more?

He'd made no count; he'd kept no score.
It had not really mattered then ...
Could it have been thus, truly been,
little more than simply dream:
illusion of a heart, grown sore,
an apparition, once he'd seen?
    In constancy, Astarte slept –

And sleeping still, she gave no sign;
no word of queen or how, her life.
If only once for him, she'd called
and given purpose to his shawl:
his shroud ... for thus it seemed.
Bereft of purpose and of queen,
he hid in darkness, growing dim:
apothecary's dream.
But still, forlorn Astarte slept,
while swain, cleft from his dreams,
    bereft ... pondered queen; her life –

Her life, he'd never questioned for,
with beauty and the joys she brought,
could not come pain with burden fraught.
How could she suffer, ever bright,
when love and beauty were her right?
In reading now, his last refrain
from long ago: a poem called 'Train' ...
he shakes with dawning and alarm;
perhaps was he, had done her harm;
had left an accidental scar,
    she carried with her from afar –

That onetime, sometime, distant past,
he'd loved, and had been loved, by her.
Could something there, have led her feet
to flee to Devon, in retreat?
Or was that verse, mere prophesy
of chance, but nothing more?
    Astarte stirs –

Foolish swain, Astarte chides.
'That you might ponder so, you're dreaming.
That you with her, could leave some meaning:
lead her somehow, to that place;
leave her in a state of grace,
longing likewise, for your face?
     You're mad! It's nothing more, than fate!'

But what if, more than poem-forsook,
it led her, to the course she took?
And coursing so, you would not know.
You thought her gone ... another's queen;
her destiny and yours, unseen.
You would have followed, had it been.
     Astarte wakes –

What is her wound, this Fisher Queen?
What hurt, what pain, what sorrow; spleen?
He senses it and feels its chill ...
the malady she suffers, still.
She flees in terror and alarm,
afraid that he, might do her, harm.
What harm was done, he cannot know –
and so, he curses mind, so slow;
so thick, that he might never grasp
the depth or meaning, of his task.
     Astarte wakes and rises –

What if the cups they seek, were one ...
both wounds, to share and overcome;
in constancy, their hurts to spare;
in loving and with caring, where
     one grail for both, becomes –

Astarte placed grails in two hearts ...
hiding them in distant parts,
waiting for the time to come,
when destiny would make as one:
    a product greater than its sum.

Seven, and-one-half, millennia of exile.
Was she there, for him to find?
Or was she only in his mind?
Was it always meant that way ...
the swain, to wander every day
and through each night, pursue his plight;
her being, always in his sight ...
    her sound ... his soul?

(A conclusion of sorts, some twenty-five years later,
to 'The Keeper', written in London, in 1975:
a conclusion which was to remain, forever un-concluded,
suspended in what Japanese Ukio-e artists would call,
'the floating world'.)

ANTELOPE DREAMS

Once again,
antelope dreams abound.
They fill my nights and days
with longing for sun-swept plains
and the soft, sweet scent of you.

Once again,
I hunger but to hear your sound:
the drumming of their hoofs to drown
and feast my eyes, with the ever-lissom
curving of your spine.

How can I sleep at all ...
again, still, or ever?
I can only watch in thrall
and walk behind you.

(A reprise of sorts, to 'London Spring',
some 25 years earlier.)

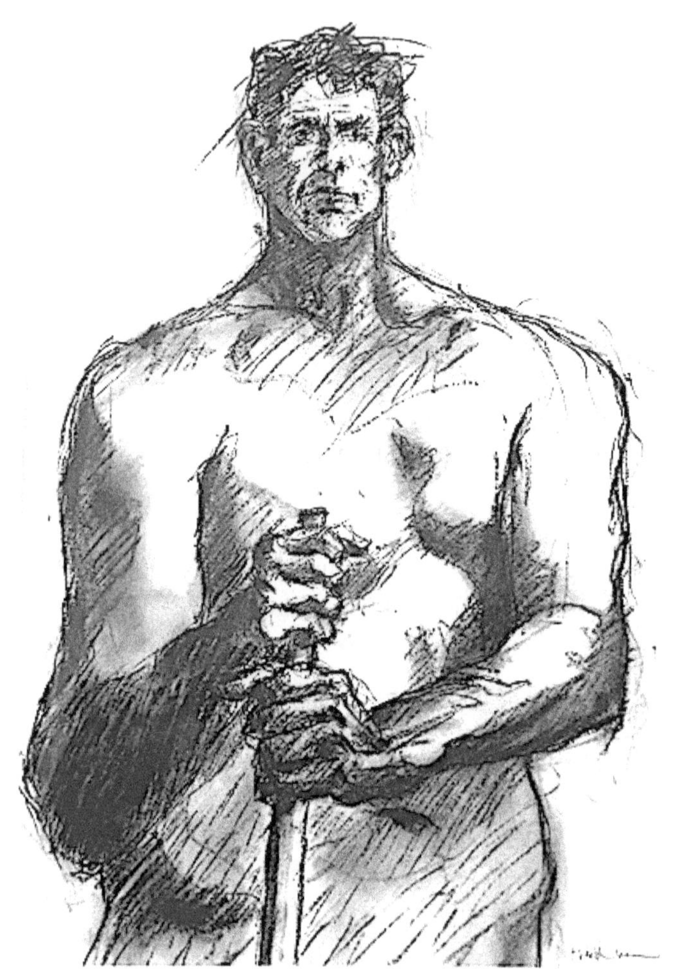

'STANDING FIGURE WITH STAFF'
Compressed charcoal on Cartridge Paper, 2009

COUPLING TANKAS: ON WAKING

For were I to gaze
upon you every day ...
New longing would stir
me afresh, with each sunrise,
resting spoon-wise by your side.

For were I to wake,
sated with last night's loving ...
Resting by your side,
head, heart and loins would quicken
to the sight and smell of you.

And were I to write
these verses every night,
upon your fair skin ...
Visions of your morning form
would urge their soft retelling.

REPRISE

With those first words,
You cleared these ears of deafness –
And forgotten yearnings stirred,
Of dreams, from nights so endless.

With that first kiss,
You woke this heart from sleeping,
Through remembered longing's mists,
Which held you in their keeping.

With that first, later coupling,
You balmed these limbs with sweetness –
Peeled back the years of suffering
And bathed with love so selfless.

With kisses, words and loving,
You've corrected this life's list –
Returned the song so long unheard;
Reclaimed for me, the joys forsaken;
Restored to me, the path once taken.

So long ago, you claimed this heart –
If claims are made, they're yours ...
You've owned them from the start.

MORNING SONG

Quicksilver morning
slipping over treetops ...
Gut-wrenching longing
holds me pinned against
these walls, sans toi.

Freshly-pressed, a Jarrett phrase
caresses face with tears:
a gentle waterfall to splash
softly, past this agony's rocks ...
while fresh-drawn coffee
steams just with a dash.

Quicksilver mourning and
my cough matches yours ...
matches yours, my fate.
Mercurial rising
pined against my walls.

I cough and reach
for another cigarette,
toi-bound, sky-bound,
thigh-bound, unbound ...
The All-claiming Key
to all life's other claims.

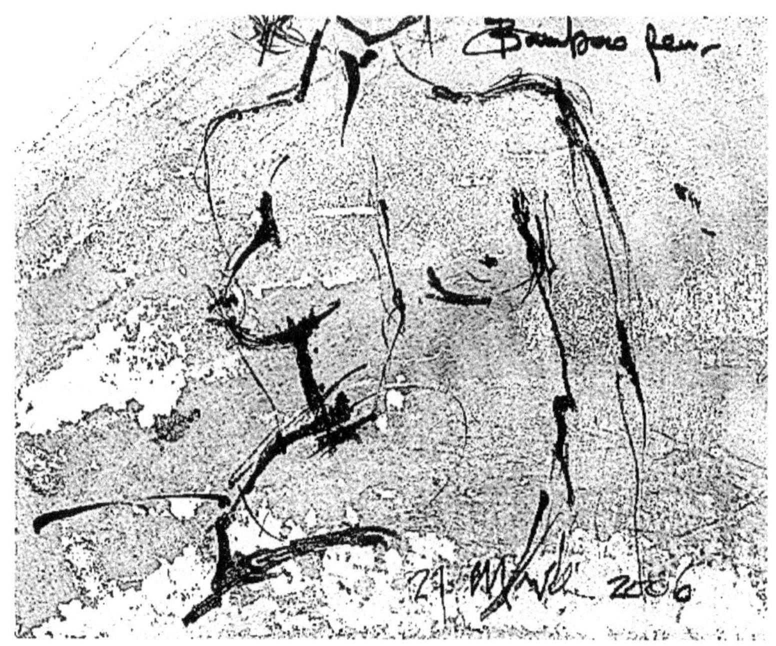

'TORSO'
Bamboo pen & Indian ink on rusted Arches Paper, 2006

THIRTY-FIVE TANKAS
OF LOSS AND DESOLATION ...

ONE TO FIVE : 24 May 2001

A cold wind blowing
Words and birds drop from branches ...
Winter already?
Empty branches break like hearts
And spring will not come again.

Chill descends on heart ...
Brel accompanies it now
And limbs grow restless.
Was it only yesterday
When love at last seemed so real?

Autumn was so short ...
Can that be snow already
When leaves are still gold?
Just an early frost swept down
From heights of aspiration.

The gods must laugh now
At such insolence ... that she
Could love him only.
Listen while his heart breaks like
Empty branches in winter.

Brel still fills his ears ...
The night is long and empty –
Winter hounds his door.
Summer and autumn are gone ...
Winter chills his aching heart.

SIX TO TEN : 25 May 2001

Icy wind beats door ...
Lights flicker, then extinguish.
Only wind remains.
Was autumn so late coming
That winter is here so soon?

A fallen flower?
No, just a crushed butterfly ...
Someone held it close.
Insects are such fragile things.
Sit still and let them alight.

Lone bird drops from sky.
A sharp crack breaks the silence ...
The last hunter's gun?
No ... a branch heavy with snow
And sound of one heart breaking.

Shaking outstretched hand
A crumpled piece of colour ...
Someone's used Kleenex?
Love's quivering butterfly
Should not be held so closely.

A muffled retort ...
Love's suicide smokes gently
And crumpled soul flees.
One poet spoke too freely
And singed the wings of freedom.

ELEVEN TO FIFTEEN : 25 May 2001

This blood heat plummets ...
Body racked with shivering
But winter in May?
The foot-shot poet shudders
As love and life seep from him.

One foot in bucket
He limps across the room and
Memories of mouth.
The poet's songs fell lifeless
At the alter of his Love.

This night is so cold ...
His bones and heart cry to him
Where is his Love's fire?
This has promise of being
A long and empty winter.

Why love's suicide
Must be inevitable
The heart cannot tell ...
Butterflies lie quivering
As evidence of clutching.

A path of Kleenex!
A great lover has walked here ...
This is evidence!
So many crushed butterflies
Testify his way with words.

SIXTEEN TO TWENTY : 26 May 2001

He recognises
That he walked this path before ...
Crushed wings litter it.
Don't clutch their wings but let them
Brush against you when ready.

An empty churchyard ...
No votive offering there
For the suicide.
The poet took his own love
With too many miss-timed words.

They said: Don't worry
She just needs a little space ...
But he knew better.
Winter winds howled at his door
And torn wings seeped under it.

A heart lies open ...
This is no operation
But a tragedy.
The poet opened his heart
Then ground down his foot in it.

Oh, luckless poet!
To wait so long for summer
And find it cancelled ...
Verses fell from high above.
Past hurts turned them to snowflakes.

TWENTY-ONE TO TWENTY-FIVE : 26 May 2001

A bare empty sky
A bald rock and a barren tree
A sharp clear coldness ...
Dirty smudge on horizon
Heralds a coming snowstorm.

In middle of night
The poet calls out her name
And the clock ticks on ...
Winds of hurt muffle his cry
And terror covers her heart.

When it's winter here
Half-world away comes summer ...
That's where she will be.
With her comes summer and spring
With him comes only the fall.

Fresh sheets are useless ...
Whatever hopes may have been ...
For an empty bed.
Just as useless are sweet words
To a heart that's torn by hurt.

Scent of butterflies
Crushed by hasty affection
Mingle with longing ...
Unpacked sheets taunt the poet
As midnight comes and passes.

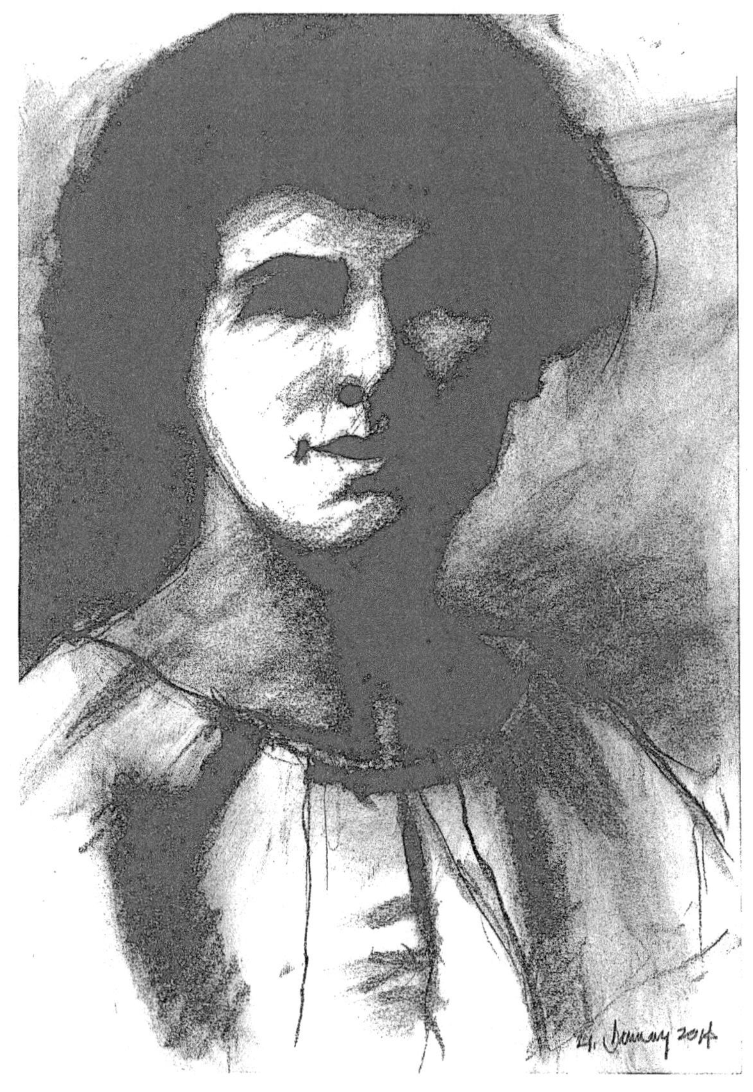

'MY GRANDMOTHER, EMMA LAVINA ASHBY'
Compressed charcoal on Cartridge Paper, 2014

TWENTY-SIX TO THIRTY : 27 May 2001

The door stands open.
He dare not nudge it for fear
That no-one is there ...
He saw the wild geese winging
And the onset of winter.

Unseasonal chill
With unreasonable fear
Freezes his movements ...
He sees the littered corpses:
These quivering butterflies.

What day can this be?
Since butterfly message came
He lost track of time ...
Is this autumn or winter
That litters the path with wings?

Alan Watts and zen
Haunt the poet's reasoning
Of why how and when ...
When is love if it's broken?
Why is hurt how lovers fear?

The zen of loving
Turns all reason, upside down
Makes fools of sages ...
When is she if she's loving?
Why is he when she's hurting?

THIRTY-ONE TO THIRTY-FIVE :
27 and 28 May 2001

New moon and stillness
Ooze under this door's threshold
Bringing heart-deep chill ...
The forecast was for such joy
And suddenly it's sleeting.

In another life
Winter came this early twice
Without forewarning ...
One would think that he should learn
To pack woollies and warm vests.

From out of clear sky
A small speck plummets earthward ...
A meteorite?
Just a small starling struck down
By winter's chill of lost love.

Winter sun on back
The poet shakes off ennui
Turns his mind to spring ...
The wild geese will then return
Bringing joys to light his nights.

Today is warmer
A chrysalis is splitting
Heralding the spring ...
Metamorphosis complete
Soft crushed wings may yet unfurl.

MY BOAT UNDER THE STARS

My boat out under the stars
has become my favourite place.
It's here, with my love's compass
I can both charter time and space ...
And when the moon is full
steer my craft by the light of your face:
Heaven's Helmsman, full of grace.

My star-boat's name is Ever ...
You are its guiding light.
As aeons spin about me
you maintain my course at night
and when no stars prevail
provide a glow, however slight ...
Heaven's Highway, clear and bright

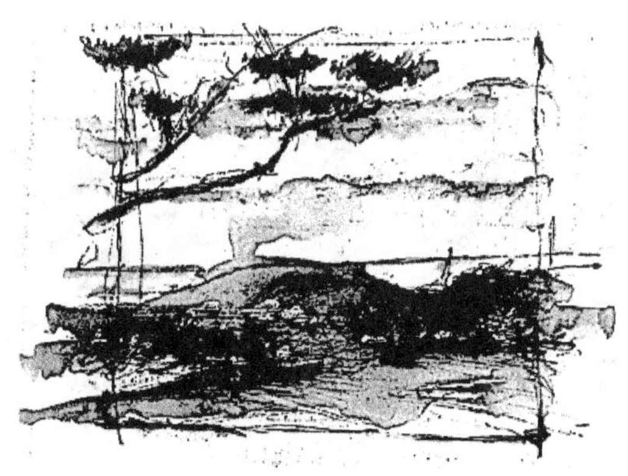

'FROM FALCONCOURT'
Rollerball & wash on Arches Paper, 2012

ENLIGHTENMENT TANKAS

With these feet on ground
With this head among the stars
I am neophyte.
Hold me, stretched from pole to pole
Centre my being with yours.

Abstraction resting
In a sky pregnant with stars ...
Boundless universe.
Once touched, the soul is boundless –
All beliefs, wrested from this.

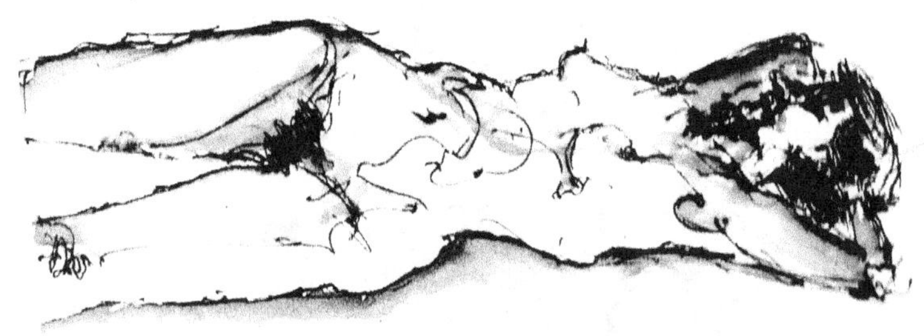

'RECLINING FIGURE'
Rollerball & wash on Arches Paper, 2007

TO THE GODDESS WITHIN

Ancient seed of sleeping sky
in vengeance, wrested from those thighs
of father, by a Titan son ...
her sickle-handed sibling.
The goddess woke and woke the world
to fearsomeness and beauty.
Deep from shell-strewn temple bounds
she reigns and walks the world
in love and beauty awesome ...
thus walking, lives the goddess
wakes within us all.

* * *

I watch the walkers
and walking thus, watch I
these margins of a surging realm
stretched wide between the shore and sky
in majesty and plumbless depths ...
mere edges of that consciousness.
I love this space, this interface
that stretches to the sky ...
so, walking thus and watching thus
walk I.

I watch in wonder
and wondering thus, watch I
the beauty of these fearsome depths
vast surging of a consciousness
released upon our sphere of being
men and gods ... mere instruments
of heaven's promptings, locked
in waking dreams and aspirations
suspended in the sky ...
so, wondering thus and dreaming thus
watch I.

When you're withdrawn and at your ebb
your temple lost in deepness ...
your soughing whispers
'I am here. This is no web
for I am resident beyond the seagull's crying.
I am your body's element, the bearer of your soul.

I am the yin, your feminine
the truth to make you whole.
I come in beauty, come in love
the content of your chalice ...
the half you lost and laid aside
your very grist and core.
I shore your soul and shoring thus
your soul, in shoaling, soars.'

REALTIME REVISITED

Realtime? Yes!
I heard it long ago and thought
it simply myth ...
a childlike fable, danger-fraught
a longing, that all good sense taught
could be no more than merely glyph.

Realtime? Yes!
I heard it ringing frequently
and thought it out of season ...
of how it could not ever be
but yet it pealed incessantly
defying ears to pause –
to doubt the gulf which seemed
so wide, that time and years
seemed to divide ...
yet realtime, will not hang about.

Realtime? Yes!
I've heard its passing in my night
and wondered if
that footstep heard, however slight
might with my soul one day, take flight ...
be more than simply gift.

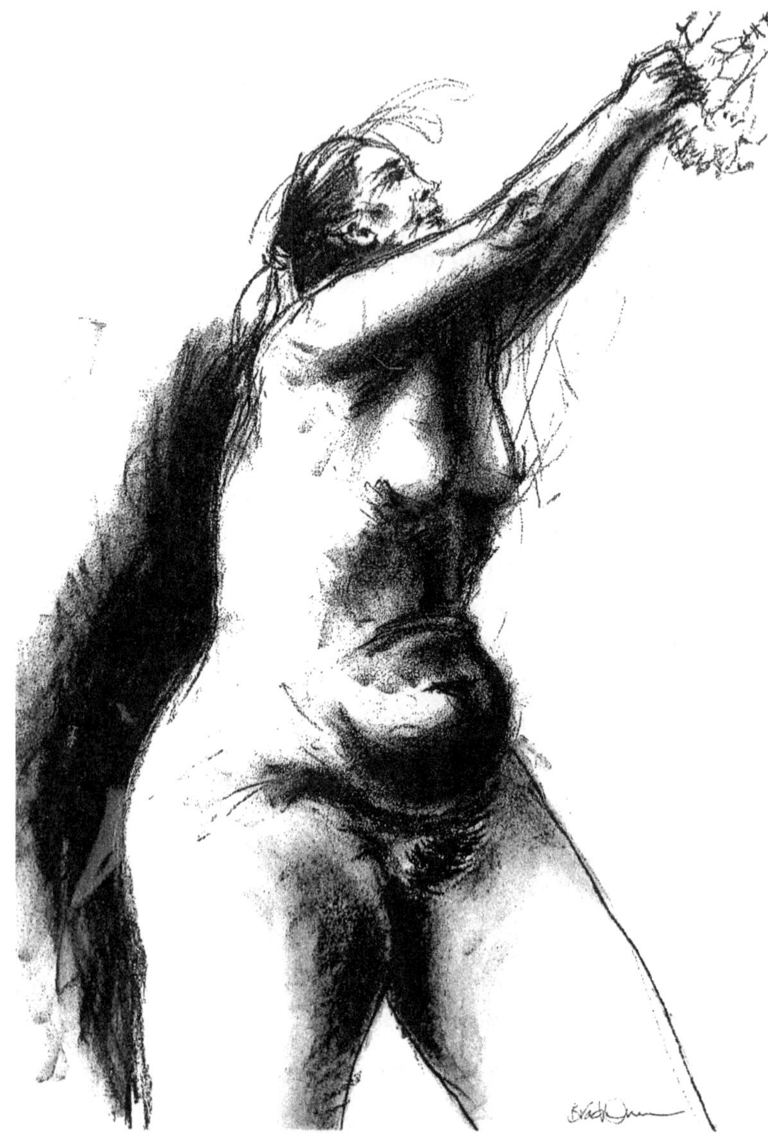

'STANDING WOMAN'

Compressed charcoal on Cartridge Paper, 2007

JACK

My sprawling Jack-of-Frost
lays on his back ... accosts
me with the tune
that hangs me from him.
He tunes the song he sings
from keepsakes lacking strings
or sounding-boards
for yesterday's illusions.

My scornful Jack-of-Frost
swings from my back and scoffs
about the lack
of rhyme or reason.
He reasons as he rants
about the obstacles of chance ...
that steeplechase
of falls and fate's contusions.

My robbing Jack-of-Grief
steals by me in my sleep
to render down
the turgid fat of reason.
He renders as he paints
from the palette time acquaints
with aching wounds
and destiny's deep lesions.

My distant Jack-of-Reason
slips inside me out of season
to spread his tendrils gently
through my spine.
He thrusts his fingers deep
beneath the tissue of my sleep ...
an alchemist
of animus confusion.

My whistling Jack-in-Season
rubs against me with good reason
as he modulates the passage of the song.
His melody now falters as its tempo gently alters
and it moves into a sometimes-minor key
of changes, chords well-tempered
diminished but augmented ...
the theme its own, defying transposition.

Of all the Jacks-that-Gather
in these days, the one that matters
most of all is that
of mocking Jack-of-Truth ...
that prince of lost illusions
and price for thought transfusions
sees life, a leap of faith
not wanting proof.

AND YET THEY THANK HER

Just another scalp, on the belt
of the goddess moving fleet-foot
through the undergrowth –
sliding through the shadows
of ghosts and summers past ...
and, silent as the mists of morning,
melt and vanish in the cold
hard light of day.

Just another pelt, to charm
the waistline of a silent sylph,
moving with a grace
that time forgot ... but not
forgotten by the bald ones
listing in her wake ...
no time could take from them
the hunger she so readily begot.

And yet they thank her
for their baldness,
listing,
hunger ...
beg her, once again
to charm their senses,
take their skin
and wear it, for her own.

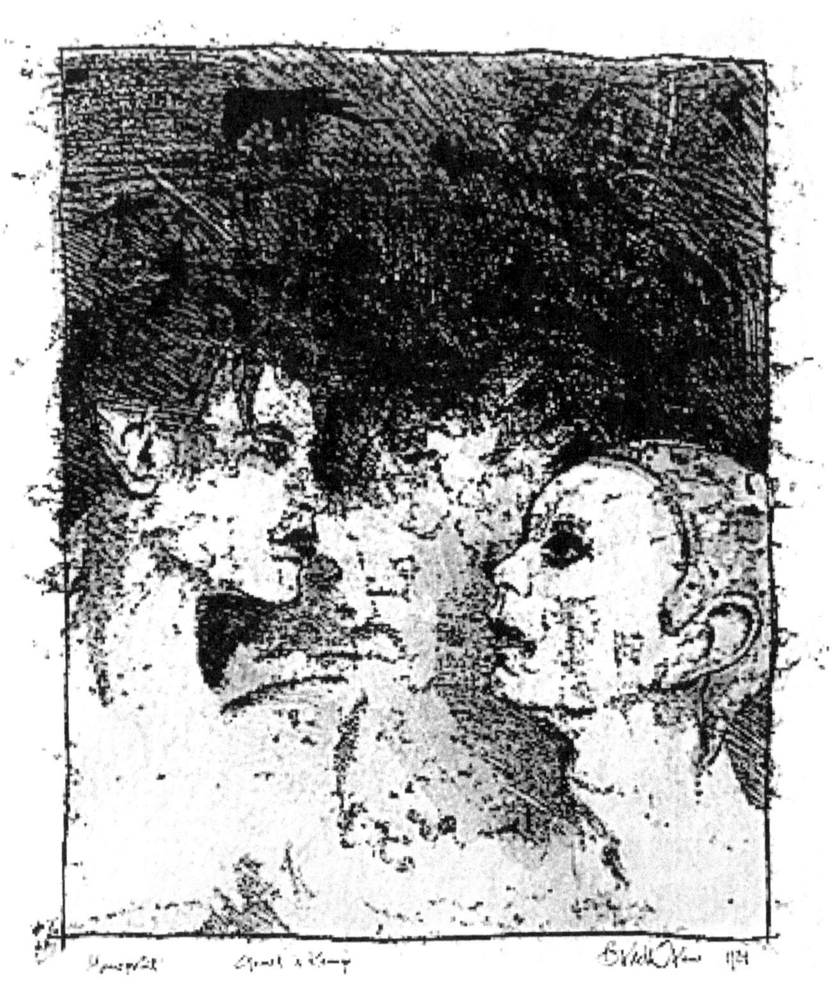

'GENET à KEMP'
Mono-print on Japanese Rice Paper, 1981
(From the coloured original)

I HAD WONDERED

I had wondered when you left
if words would dry
like leaves before their falling ...
If like the thoughts
would tongue be cleft
and left to flounder, as some wreck
stranded on the shoals
of summer's passage.

I have wondered with you gone
if thoughts would fly
like leaves at autumn's calling ...
If with its call
would end our song
as might migrate the noble swan
leaving at the first
grey hint of winter.

I have wondered in your void
if tongue would tie
like bells bereft of tolling ...
If in that lull
of peal devoid
few means might be deployed
to warn of danger ...
Save life's barge from shoaling.

For I have laboured in your wake
my voice to fly ... this thirst to slake ...
The beast to name that in my waking
hunts me in this undertaking
breathing down my neck and days
intent to rob from me that tune
hanging from my voice, consumed
by self-defeating torpor.

But I will yield no satisfaction
for the beast thrives on inaction.
The roots and fruits his thrusting snout
grub out, are those of faith and doubt ...
the faith to love, the doubt to leave ...
Twin yarns in the magician's sleeve
best separated on the loom
by reconfiguring fate's tune.

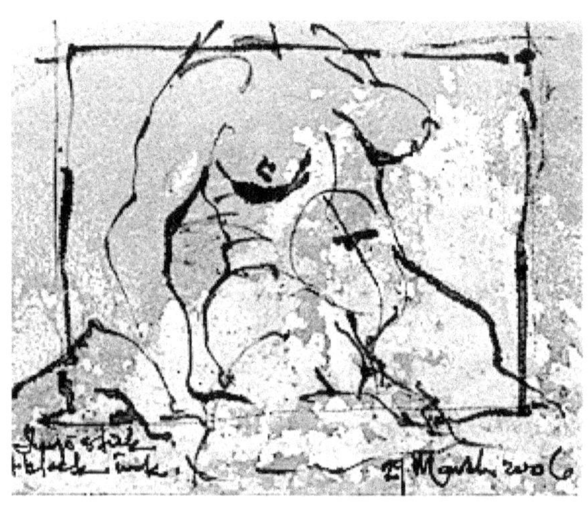

'TORSO No.2'
Sharpened stick & Indian ink on rusted Arches Paper, 2006

TANKAS:
REQUIEM FOR A GODDESS

Standing in the waste
Where scattered hearts lie fractured
Gleaming at her feet –
The stage lies empty, soundless ...
Footlights dimmed, the cast has left.

When all that is left
Is grey of autumn's dreaming –
What will it matter
How adoration flattered
When the gods and beauty fly?

A lonely runner
Pounds the life-long pavement course
Running for her life ...
For or from, is the question.
Is she chasing or fleeing?

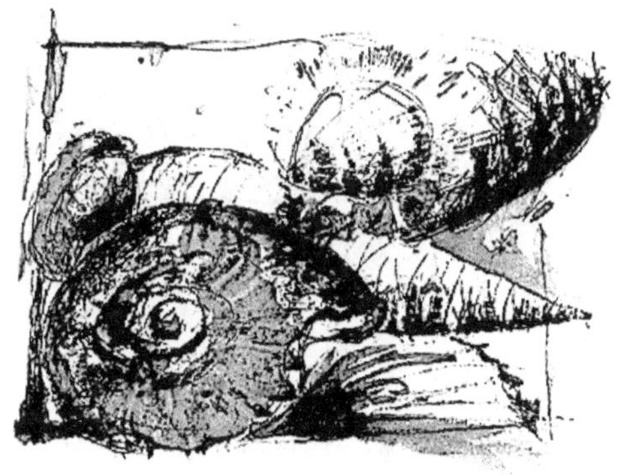

'SUSAN'S SHELLS'
Rollerball & wash on Arches Paper, 2006

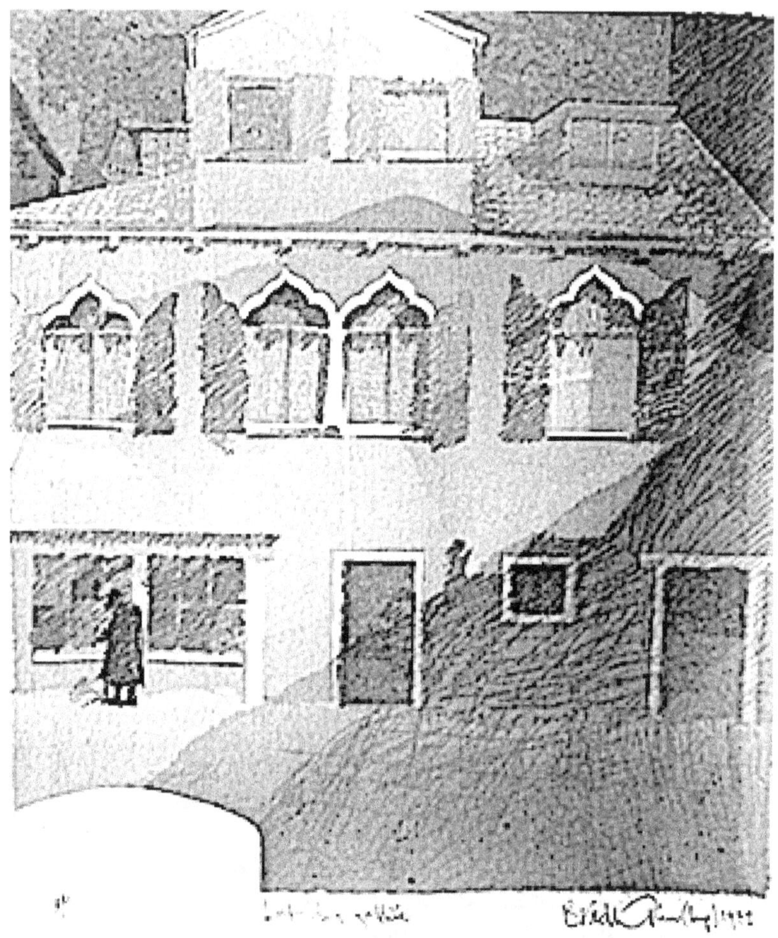

'LOST DOG GOTHIC'
Screenprint on Arches Dessin Paper, 1982
(From the full-colour original)

BLACKALL RANGE
JULY 2003 TO MARCH 2016

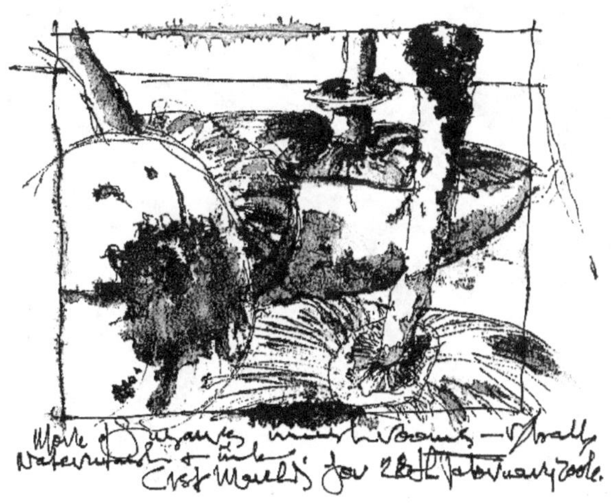

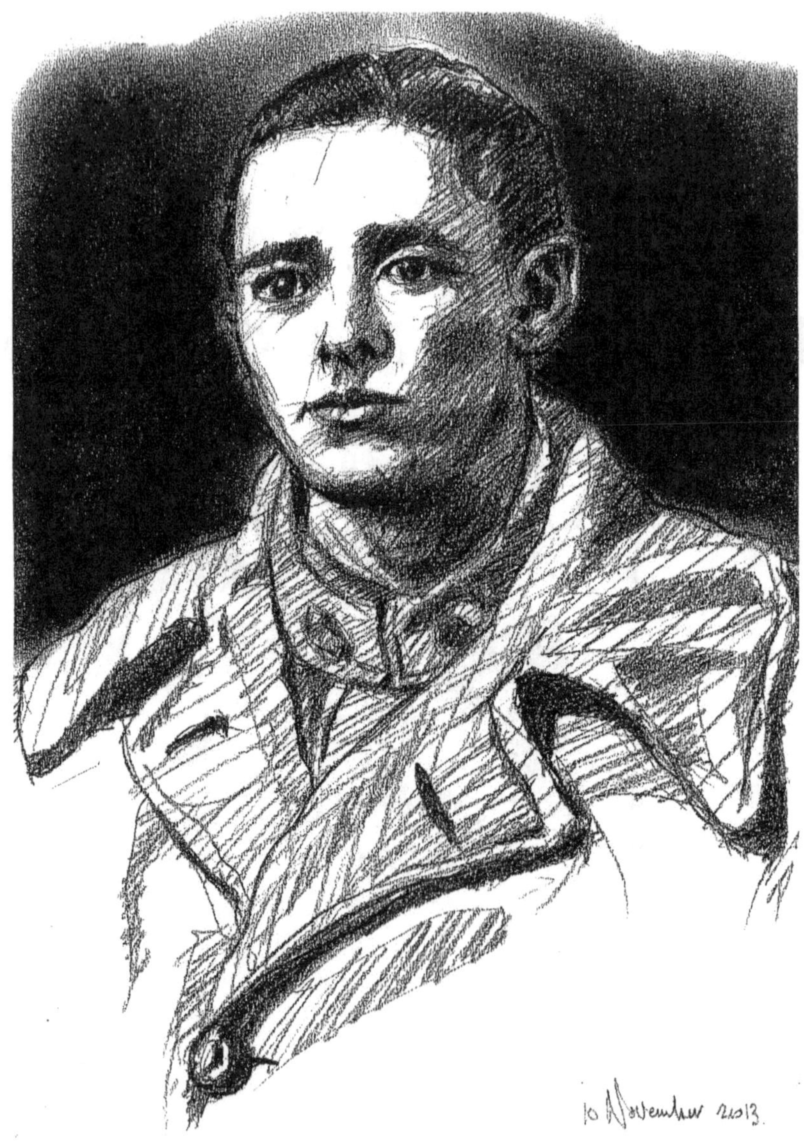

'MY GRANDFATHER, HERBERT DREW, 1915'
Conte crayon & compressed charcoal on Cartridge Paper, 2013

MORNING PAGES

In the stillness
and the breaking of the night,
stars wink out and daylight hums,
to draw from sleep, put dreams to flight.
The book lies open ... this day's life
awaiting substance from its source ...
to draw from dreams, a present course.

Hordes throng the gates ...
the audience is restless,
all tickets paid; the cast arrayed
in all their tatty splendour.
Both living and the dead cry out,
seek recognition from past doubts ...
their meaning, cause, their tenure;
the mundane duties, must-be-dones;
the hopes, the dreams, the pleasures.

Aches and longings hang at bay,
aspirations pending ...
the quest remains still-veiled in haze,
its story, never-ending.
Procrastination clouds the mind,
prevarication circling;
the clamour and the din increase ...
Where's comprehension, bringing peace?

In the awkwardness
and finality of silence ...
the thoughts won't stop,
while words won't come,
to still the brain's incessant hum.

MOONSHINE ALLEY

Almost moonshine alley ...
and the clunking bamboo clatter
of the wind-chime stills the air
that drives the scudding white caps
through the sky ...

And hair that ruffles
in the madness of the flight
down firefly highways
with the words that none dare whisper
to the night.

Listing moonshine galley
where staccato tree-frogs stammer
as the wind-chime fills the air
that drives the scudding memories
from the sky ...

And fear that scuffles
with the sadness of the flight
of gadfly byways
and the thoughts that come unbidden
to the night ...

Where thirsting memory mingles
with present tense ... the sense
that all things started and abandoned
to that flight, fell in a time
when all seemed ripe

And ready to the touch of discontent ...
when beckoning firefly highways
gave way to gadfly byways
while meaningless distractions
drowned the air.

Almost moonshine alley ...
and the cheerful bamboo chatter
of the wind-chime clears the air
that drives the scudding whitecaps
through the sky ...

And hair that ruffles
in the gladness of the flight
of firefly highways
with the thoughts that one dares whisper
to the night.

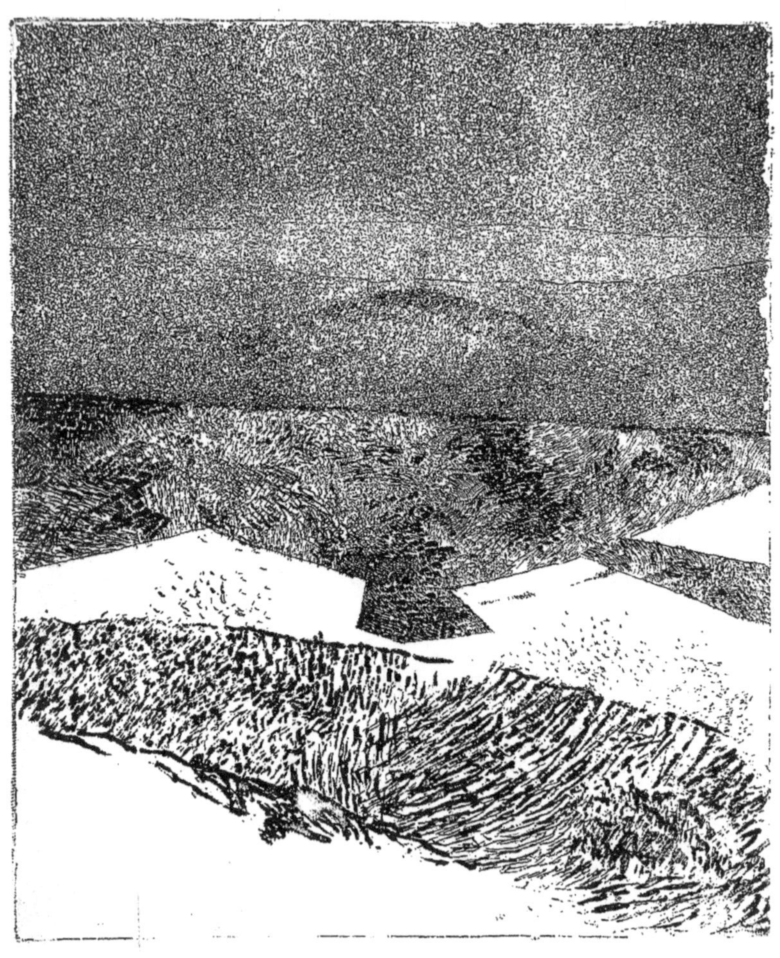

'FROM BALD KNOB'
Zinc plate etching on Rag Paper, 1980

DOWNPOUR IN THE CITY

Downpour in the city ...
and the solitary rainspout swells to overflowing;
spews its overburden with no discrimination;
cuts a swathe that parts the wave
of lemming-borne umbrellas
beating their hasty crocodile retreat
from this sudden
and most-unseasonable deluge.

Friday afternoon and a downpour in the city ...
the drumming din drowns out the traffic roar,
the maitre d', all idle conversation.
Lovers huddle in sodden intimacy
along the café margins
and downwind of the deluge,
trapped against the surging lemming tide
in abrupt but not unwelcome togetherness.

Hardly-hidden headlamps flaring,
skinny girls blaze their way toward a virgin destiny;
while grim-faced shoppers,
Christmas clutched in one free arm,
brave the tide and scuttle
in a rush none understands ...
Basic seasonal programming
for scuttle bugs to wend and weave their tenuous way ...
And still, the rainspout giant pisses on.

Accents jostle with the downpour din ...
solemn matriarchs with spouse in tow
(all imports from some other place)
emerge in mild bewilderment,
intents at promenade now foiled.
Large-nosed girls, small breasts and teasing eyes
aflame with matching egos, breast this tide
to dance the tourist tango.

This is glorious!
Buenos Aires must have been like this
when cafes thronged and spilled the streets;
while sudden and unseasonable downpours
fed to fill the urgency of life;
when poets and rebels mingled with the heady
sweaty smell of rushing Friday afternoons;
pungent coffee, cigarettes,
sudden rain and mobsters.

The cast and faces have not changed ...
dark-suited businessmen, intent and sombre
feign ignorance of rain, so focussed on their goals.
The timid girls with teasing eyes
dance and weave their breasting way
from an anonymous future;
while tourist matrons, spouse a-tow
(parcel-packing firsts of Season's Shoppers)
brave the dance of Friday city flights ...
And still, the solitary giant pisses on.

AND IF I WERE ...

And if I were to take this tale;
Write it, such as gods might pale
In all their bland uncertainty
That men may feel these things ...

That centuries might claim their genes,
Fill them with recurring themes
Of madness and of vision ...

Here in seeming non-avail, I hover ...
Life and love withstanding,
Lodged between the darkness
And the light.

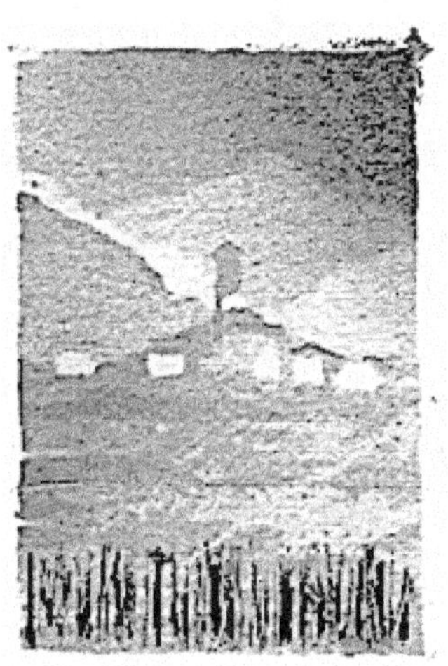

'ALPINE VILLAGE'
Screenprint on Arches Dessin Paper, 1982

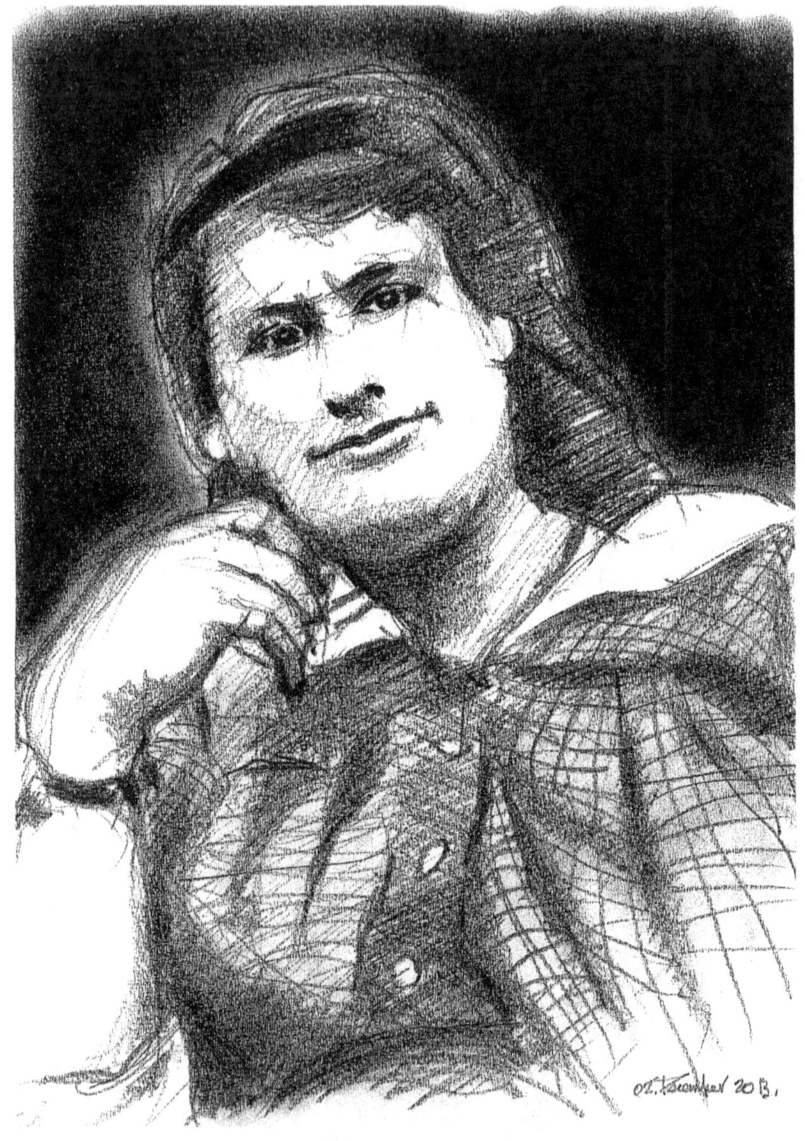

'MY GRANDMOTHER, ELIZABETH PRICE HIGGENSON, c.1915'
Conte crayon & charcoal on Cartridge Paper, 2013

AS GRIEF'S FOR LOSS ...

As Grief's for loss, so Grief's a cross to bear
Through autumn's dreaming days, a course to share ...
Thus dreaming, grieve the passing of the years;
Of friends, of youth, the wellspring's hopes and fears;
'Til Grief herself becomes too much to bear –
Engenders silence, thus to stem despair ...
Suspend the fall, the plight of flailing nights
Which Grief bestows on all whom she ignites.

Thus grieved we all, the silent mute: the wall
Pain raised about as rampart to your fear ...
Not for yourself but for the ones held dear;
And silenced thus, a clotted sanguine thrall
Plied hidden bindings and with gag replete,
Enforced a stillness as such griefs accrete ...
Consigned to rest within a living tomb;
Endure faux death, in antiseptic gloom.

There in the stillness, by such silence wrought
Where sight and sound alone, accompany thought ...
And gates are shut on all which might be said;
Where living bodies masquerade as dead;
Where well-meant smiles deny what might be real;
Unshielded words let slip despite all zeal ...
Taunt, torture, torment, slip the knot of hope;
Locked eyes, lashed ears ... the bounds of your world's scope.

* * *

To languish not between two worlds to hang
But storm the ramparts of the blood that sang
Your grief to sleep the dream of no avail ...
You summoned up your willpower to prevail
And loose the bonds which held you in their keep;
Turn back the flood which fevered sanguine sleep ...
When grief alone is all that's left to ply
Some hope must filter through, to death decry.

To fade not through insistent failing night
One spark alone was all it took to fight;
Regain a hold on all your joys held dear;
Turn back the flood of Grief with purpose clear
And garner up a host of precious hours ...
But was it just for your joy or for ours
That time and tide retreated with those years
In laughter more than in the stead of tears?

Retreat they did in part but part alone
As if the world in full could not atone;
Wipe out each blemish writ on history's page;
More hurts than could a second chance assuage ...
So passed your time in anguish mixed with joy;
Self-laughter as the means to now deploy
To see your life (all lives), some cosmic joke
Endured by all who labour in its yoke ...

And nearing end, the substance of those years
Amount to what? Some hopes, some joys, some fears;
Some aspirations never to be gained?
What cosmic joke imperfectly-explained?

What might we take when all is swept away
And clouds roll back to show us our last day?
The stage is hushed; there will be no encore ...
So came your time in time ... then nothing more.

* * *

As Grief's to part, so Grief's the heart we bared
Upon your leaving for the times unshared;
Lost to the past, lost to the times to come;
Grief is the loss to which the rest succumb.
It's for the void, the absence and the fear;
The taking for a reason still unclear;
The why and wherefore of our little lives ...
The where and how and what? ... we hope, survives.

(Dedicated to my mother's courage, determination
and resilience in the playing out of her last years.)

SUMMER HAIKU, MT NEBO

Still, hot, dawn haze sings
chirping Mexican hat-wave –
Cicada chorus.

MAPLETON DAWN

Silence is roaring
on my still hill this morning –
A hot day coming?

FINGAL FEBRUARY 2004

Sullen scrub stillness –
Shimmering blue bowers bring
butterfly blessings.

AUTUMN TANKA

Approaching autumn,
leaves and blossoms still burst forth
on trees near my home –
Fruit ripening, leaves falling
and still, fresh new growth arrives.

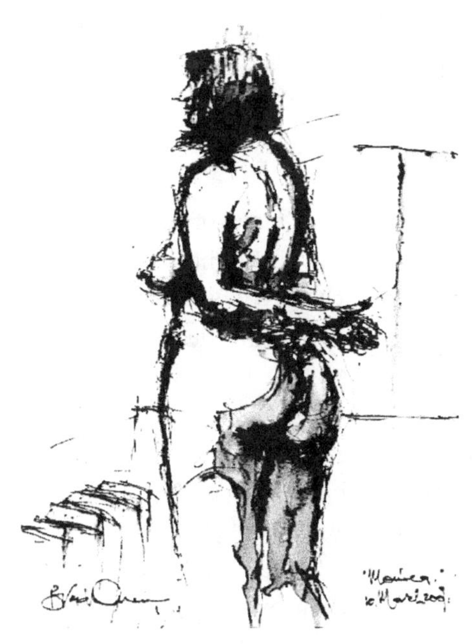

'CONTEMPLATIVE FIGURE'
Rollerball & wash on Arches Paper, 2007

A SONG OF YEARNING

In the belly of the world
there sleeps a dream they but forgot.
The world remembers, knows and dreams ...
a dream-song spun from star to stream;
in shifting grass, the stillness of
a perfect dusk and dawn-washed clouds ...
the very breath of being.

Being ... of a shifting dream
that all remember, save those in reason bred ...
in resonance of reason
one waking dream forgot.
And darkness builds ...
ten thousand thousand frames of light
in cities' darkness glowing bright;
containments of each lost soul's dream
that stillness in night's depth redeems.

In solitude they hear it yet ...
the unsaid yearning, sense of loss;
that something all have but forgot.
Behind each window, glowing bright
lone shadows move, linked by the night
and stirrings of vague memory
of what? ... they know not what it meant,
before the fall, from consciousness and grace.

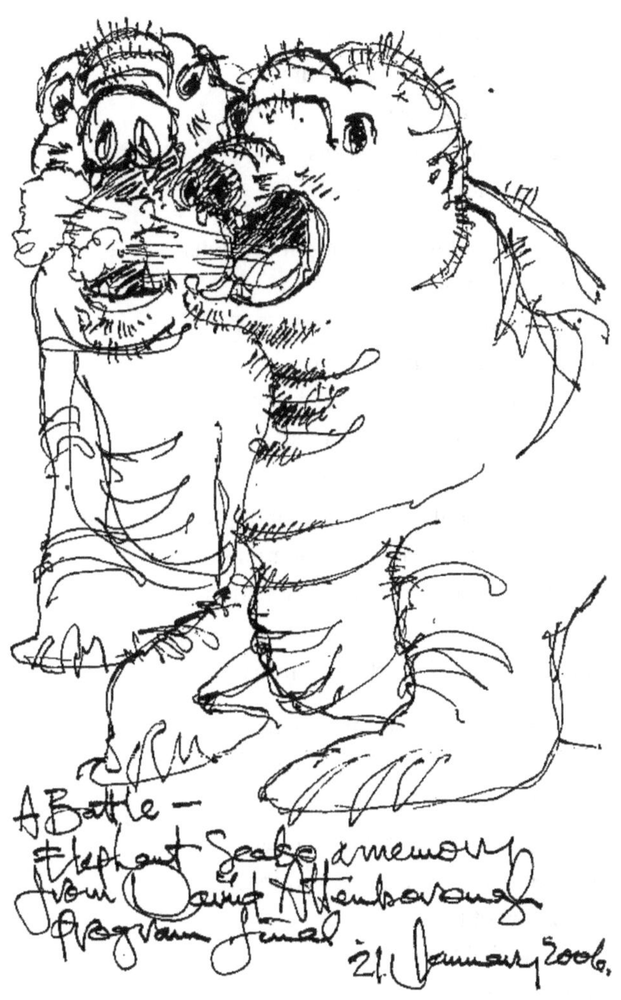

'ELEPHANT SEALS'
Rollerball on Arches Paper, 2006

CONTRAST THIS WAVE

Contrast this wave of subsea spawning
rushing to a shore still dawning ...
Surging promises of doom
visited on third-world shores
left its mark for evermore.

Homes and holdings, scant but precious
swept aside in tidal rush
and as the kraken retrogresses
remnants wallow in the slush.
But Oh! But Oh! The human cost ...
The lives in one wet moment lost!
The final score defies the count
as hundreds in their thousands mount.
The world-heard cries of inundations
thrown out from earth's poorest nations
shocks the ear, the heart, the mind ...
And still, the final death-toll climbs.

Contrast this wave, the aftermath ...
As nations of the world take heart
rush assistance, gifts of aid
to lands laid bare by sea-born swathe ...
Save pestilence, wet-filth and thirst;
the horrors of the dead
the first to feel the rigours.
Calm descends ... A people stunned
count their dead, collect possessions;
so little left from little ...
And simple lives so simply lost;
lost forever in the wash
of one great sweeping ripple.

Contrast this wave, this subsea spawn ...
Contrast this storm whose wave was born
to contrast brave humanity
whose home became an inland sea
locked by levees, might and substance ...
Still none might redeem them.

This no surging behemoth
but harpies venting all their wrath;
this storm swept all before her ...
A yielding ocean gaining strength
suppliant, followed down the length
of that great southern seaboard.
Prepared they were, precautions taken;
yet helpless still, stood by the nation
watching devastation taking hold ...
Whilst hundreds, in their thousands fled
still many, in their thousands dead
were taken to the fold.

Contrast this wave, the days that follow ...
The great man in sweet torpor wallows
waiting for his moment.
In arrogance, he waits their plea
whose home became an inland sea ...
And Oh! And Oh! The country's cost;
the property and oil drums lost!
Looting, plunder, rape and death
bestowed on those the waters left.
Land of Plenty! Home of The Free!
Is this then Prosper's Legacy ...
To foster Greed and Anarchy?

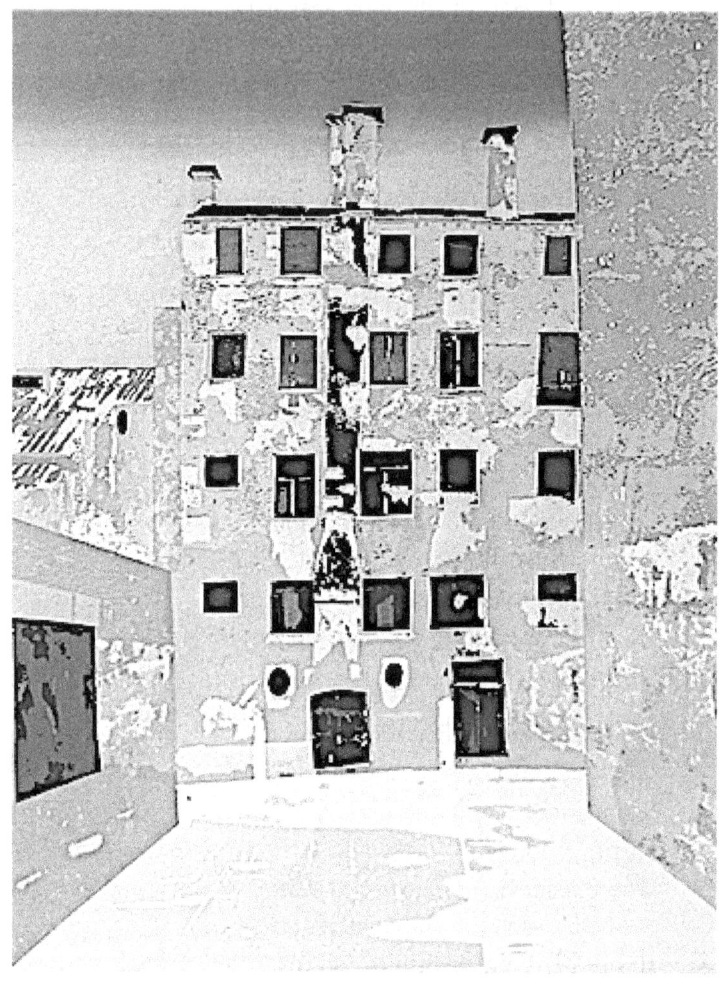

'IN A CORNER OF VENICE'
Screenprint on Arches Dessin paper, 1983
(From the full-colour original)

IN THE AFTERMATH

In the aftermath of plenty
all the citadels of plenty fall
in clouds of death from which none crawl ...
Save those to wail and beat the breast, to cry
that justice must be done and justly so;
for innocents, (not innocence)
were lost today ...
And innocents shall lose tomorrow.

In the aftermath of reason
all the gods of reason gone ...
A brooding world in madness waiting
breeding such an undertaking;
the paper house of cards imploded
as petals of decay unfolded;
stamens of their host left crying;
heartbeat of a culture dying ...
Pandemic feasting on its host
as congress prayed to Holy Ghost ...
And ganglions have taken hold,
in prophesies so long foretold
that thus, would end an era.

* * *

In the aftermath of horror
all barriers to horror fall
as packages of death arrive
in dust, designed to over-ride
complacency and safety ...
The die-hard message rolls with ease;
the media inured, to please
their audience of cult.
In the aftermath of avarice
its culture long-distended
to bursting-point; the strong anoint
the 'have' and 'have-nots' singled out
with lines of want and wanting-not
defying comprehension ...
It's no small wonder that this plunder
drives our earth with all its worth
to melt-down paranoia.

* * *

In the aftermath of carnage
all vetoes placed on carnage fail ...
So might and freedom may prevail;
protect the world from further actions
practiced by ungodly factions –
pimpernels in purdah.
The coalition's hounds unleashed
while stakes at play are now increased;
with theories of intrigue abounding
preys they seek, elude their hounding.
Resources tried, in vain they seek
to trap him like a lover, who
when passion as it does, grows weak
shape-changes to another.

* * *

In the aftermath of passion
all first flush of passion fades ...
A brave new venue fills blue screens
with vision of night raids.
A brave new villain takes the stage
the focus of this footage;
game-boy war-games, nightly played ...
No weapons found, the fiend's displayed
dragged out from ravaged wreckage.
And vindicated now, they claim
(mythologies glossed over)
reluctant order is maintained;
an interim, so highly strained
as victors take possession

* * *

In the aftermath of victory
all sweet smell of victory flies ...
A new world order, friable
fends off hints of lies.
In righteousness, the gods take seat
to meet once more at summit's peak;
assess the threat of terror ...
And terror strikes once more, again –
its echoes tremor through the glen ...
Such was expected, just not when.
Thus galvanised, cold blood in thighs,
strict measures must be rendered:
quell all freedoms which give rise
to incidents most-dreaded.

* * *

In the aftermath of terror,
all footholds found in freedom, slide ...
Most citizens have naught to fear
if citizens have naught to hide ...
Save those who fail and pay the cost
of freedoms (for protection) lost ...
To languish in Orwellian dreams ...
This world, no longer what once seemed.

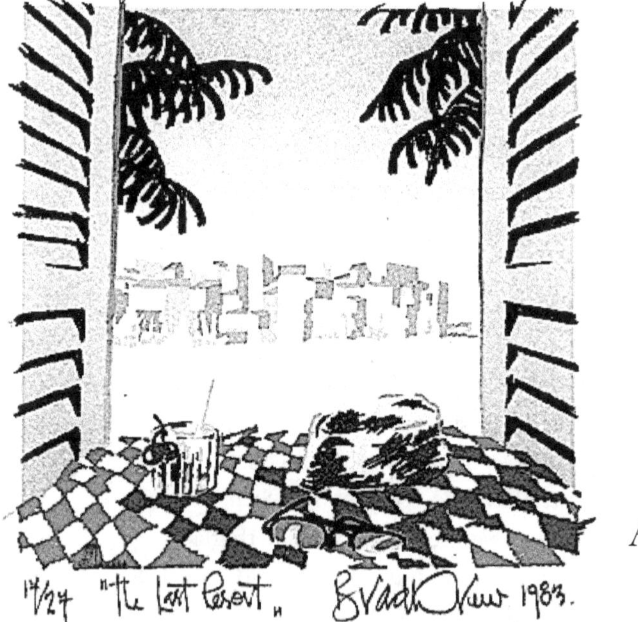

'THE LAST RESORT'
Screenprint on Arches Dessin Paper, 1983
(From the full-colour original)

A PLAY ON PLAY

Oh! We are both quite mad, we said ...
The thoughts that whisper through our head;
The urge to make of words some play
Of fancy, fact, or simply fun;
To ponder on the perfect pun ...

To rut about in rhyme and reason
Shooting rhythm out of season;
Stalking down the mind-shy stanzas
Seeking questions in the answers;
Hunting our elusive prey ...
But where's the profit line, you say?

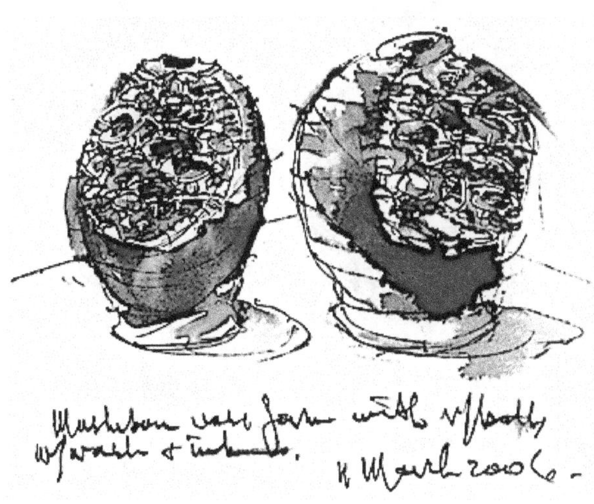

"MUSHROOM VASE"
Rollerball & wash on Arches Paper, 2006

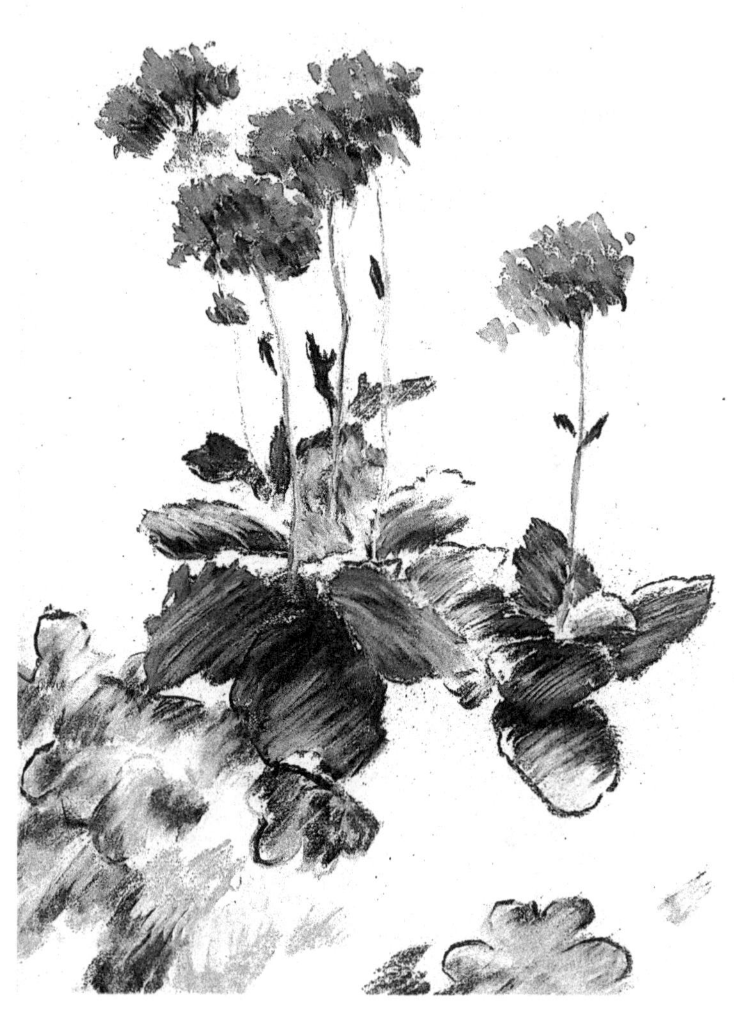

'POTTED PLANT', MT GRAVATT
Pastel on Cartridge Paper, 1977
(From the full-colour original)

GEISHA TANKA

By darkness profiled:
Beauty in the cinema
And soft scent lingers.
She weeps and touches her eye ...
Sweet ukiyo-e moment.

ON RAINY AFTERNOONS

Some rainy fog-swathed afternoons
when all is bound in silence
save muffled patters, as the leaves
sound through thickened air

with branches sighing,
stirred by breezes hardly-there –
save these, the only sound ...
one's heartbeat, keeping time.

And time stands still, embraces all
the time one ever had ... and more.

IT CAME UPON A MIDNIGHT CLEAR

It came upon a midnight clear
in hidden hymning, psalms and silent litany
arising from the hearts of men
unbidden and unvoiced ... lest doubt and fear
should seize their hearts, should hold dominion;
make of their might a mockery ...

The very gifts that set them free
to squander Man's impunity;
fragile rights that they in freedom
took for granted, held so dear
that none but gods should beg their pardon;
of no thing else have cause for fear.

It came upon a midnight clear
from dawn 'til midnight, media's means
flood the senses, fill mute heads
with doom-fraught litanies of fear ...
pandemics, bombings, siren screams
exhort the world to fear and dread.

* * *

Awakened by the fear Man's bred,
an Earth alive (Man treats as dead) ...
alive with power to end his scheming;
end the misuse, lack of care
and caring not for sirens screaming
stirs, her warning to declare ...

'If fear and terror form Man's focus
so, they should embrace his locus ...
From the barrel springs the fuse
that Man might use and so abuse
this Earth which holds him dearly ...
To the well-spring, hangs the rope
that Man might use to draw up hope;
to mend his Earth sincerely.'

* * *

It came upon a midnight clear ...
These times when fear all else outsells;
makes it a tool laconic ...
from pills and potions, household spells;
to losing freedoms, rights held dear,
through forging rules draconic.

Fear is an instinct, in its place
essential to the human race
(and every other creature)
but common use to sell coercion
every day, in every version
haunts Man's very culture.

It's gross misuse from pole to soul
creates a world no longer whole.
In the portal sits the key
all men may use to set all free;
to mend this world completely ...
In the Earth resides the power
to drive the miscreant from his tower;
re-form the world discreetly.

* * *

It came upon a midnight clear
that Man should sing a song of grace;
own his fear and wear it with his clothing ...
give it back its rightful place;
its image on cave walls adhere;
accepted free of loathing.

If fear's misuse could be reduced
Man's mother Earth might be induced
to still her restless stirring ...
Reality's what Man creates
wherein his focus most relates
with images recurring.

* * *

So sing upon a midnight clear
a theme, the image to maintain
of faith in joy and beauty ...
Faith in the well-spring, to sustain ...
Belief in the emboldened duty
to cherish Earth and hold her dearly –
proclaiming to the midnight clearly ...
There's naught to fear on Earth but fear.

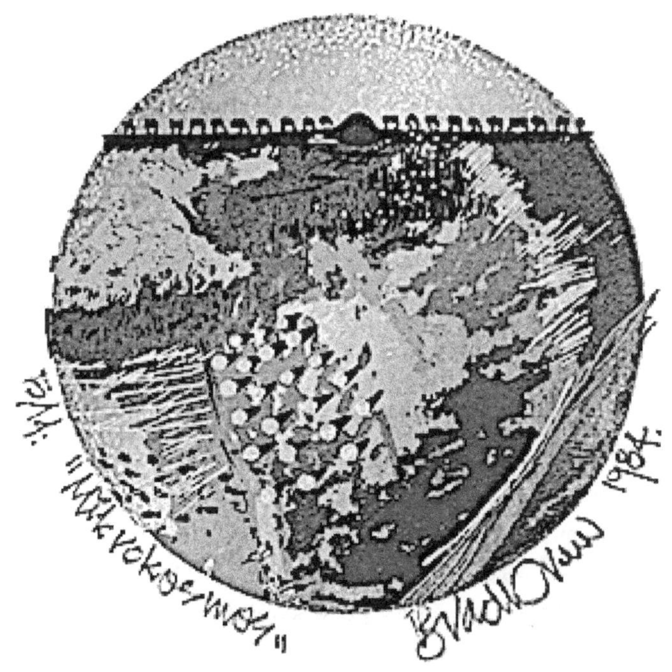

'MICROCOSMOS'
Screenprint on Arches Dessin Paper, 1984
((From the full-colour original)

TIME SLIPS THE WARP

Time slips the warp where time and timely place
co-mingle on the loom of space laid bare
and each thread slips the cloth where shadows fade
(the world seen edgewise in a strand of hair).
On my event horizon's interface
what now seems convex was before, concave ...
and all good reason and good sense efface.

Twice paradoxed within a field of grace
twin singularities urge dreams to dare
and each dream slips the cloth that time upbraids
(the world lost edgewise in a dark-sunned pair).
On my event horizon's interface
all shadows cast and passed in space-time fade ...
and all good reason and good sense efface.

Time slips the warp wherein your voice relates
co-mingling on the loom that fate lays bare
and each word slips the cloth where dreams reside
(illusion lodging in a place none dares).
On my event horizon's interface
all boundaries of space and time subside ...
each moment merging at one point of grace.

Twinned irises with depths where time abates
turn in a dance no quantum could prepare
and each step strips the cloth, its fabric frayed
(the fool's an angel lacking cause to care).
On my event horizon's interface
assumptions of what's probable abrade ...
and all good reason and good sense efface.

Time slips the warp where time and seemly grace
entangle on the loom of space laid bare
and each move shifts the cloth the wise evade
(the fool lifts shadows where none others dare).
On my event horizon's interface
the vortex dancing in your eyes persuades
to all good reason and good sense efface.

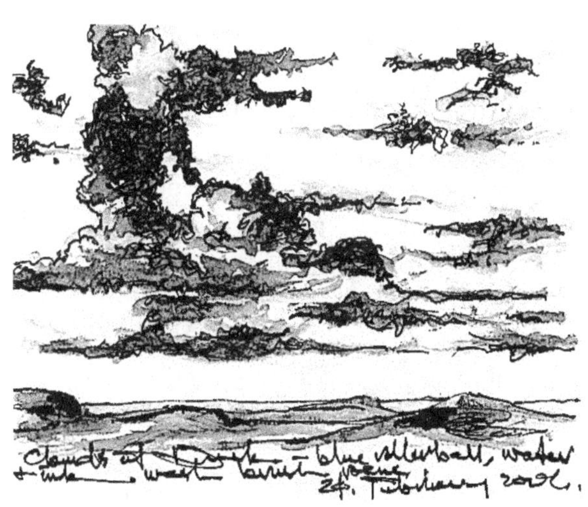

'CLOUDS AT DUSK, FALCONCOURT'
Rollerball & wash on Arches Paper, 2006

MUTE CELLS CRY OUT

Mute cells cry out to catch again the dew,
call out the dawn to free the fleeting night
as mute, they throng among the blessed few.

In silence, led by thirsts as they accrue
in waiting on this first spring blush of light,
mute cells cry out to catch again the dew.

Dawn garners hope to feed the pulse, pursue
the promised hint of winter in its flight
as mute, they throng among the blessed few ...

lean hillsides rush to herald with their hue,
spring's flush, as growing in their purpose, might
mute cells cry out to catch again the dew

and parched thirsts drink, neglected cells imbue
the residues of winter in its flight,
as mute, they throng among the blessed few.

Should seasons fail, their bright gifts then eschew ...
still calling for a cause to give delight,
mute cells cry out to catch again the dew

and urge the hillsides not to once subdue
relief they found an instant in their sight
as mute, they throng among the blessed few.

While patiently, they wait again their cue
to welcome in a spring ablaze with might,
mute cells cry out to catch again the dew
as mute, they throng among the blessed few.

(An extended villanelle)

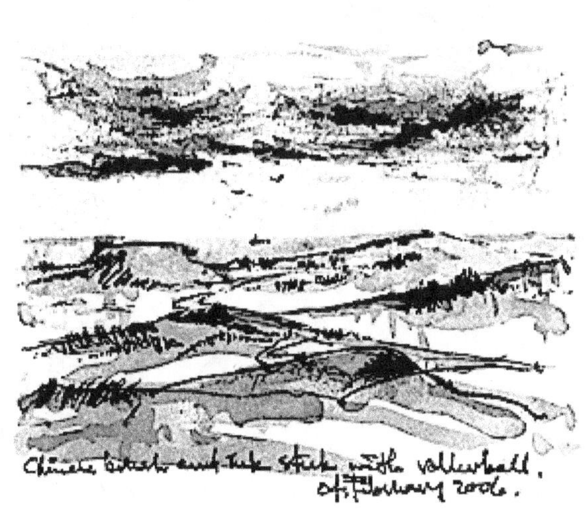

'MY FALCONCOURT OUTLOOK'
Chinese brush & rollerball on Arches Paper, 2006

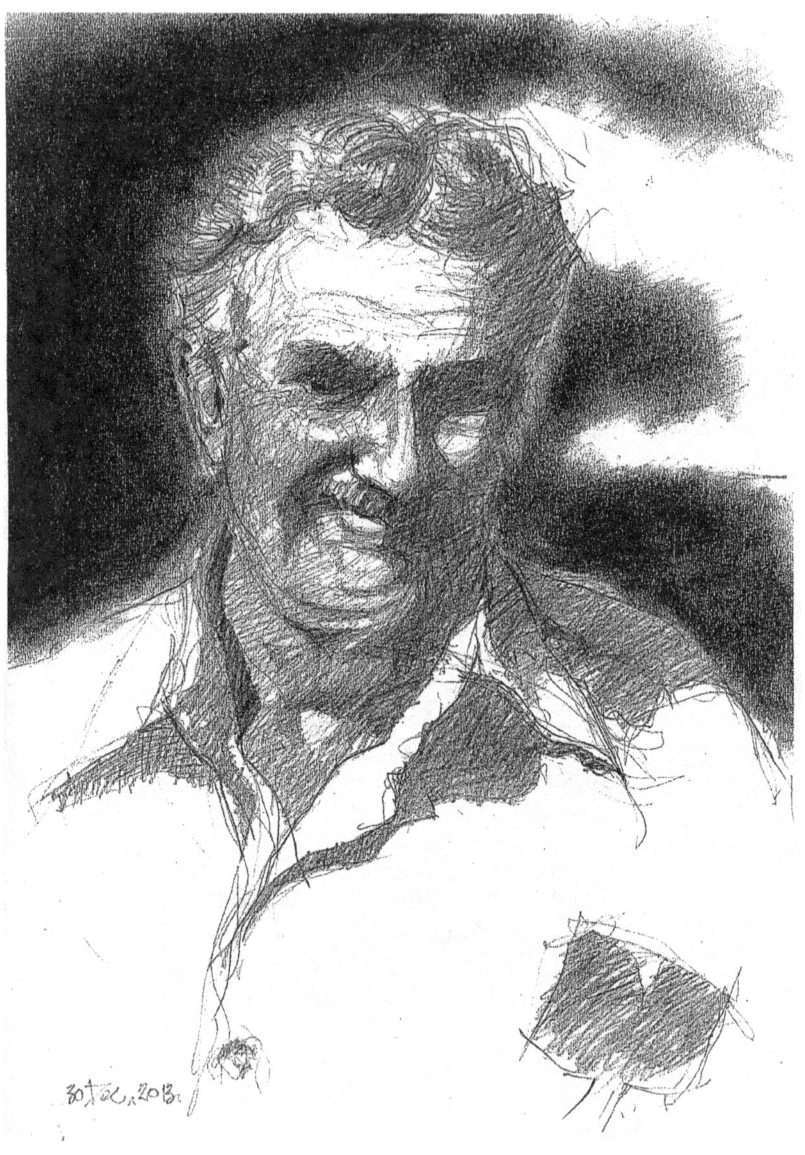

'TEDDY TANNER'
Graphite block & charcoal on Cartridge Paper, 2013

WHAT CAUSED THE STATESMEN ALL

What caused the statesmen all, to go away;
to leave affairs of state to rogues and fools
who build a future tainted by dismay,
foresight and wisdom absent from their tools?
What left us with so very little choice;
who at the ballots, is there to give hope
and through the shadows, guide us by their voice,
 convince us of ability to cope?

Well-meaning men, believing they could fly
and finish hard, the race they chose to run,
too late have found they ventured far too high,
their feathers softened, broken by the sun.
Where are the men of substance at the helm
whom greed or vanity shan't overwhelm?

(A Shakespearean sonnet)

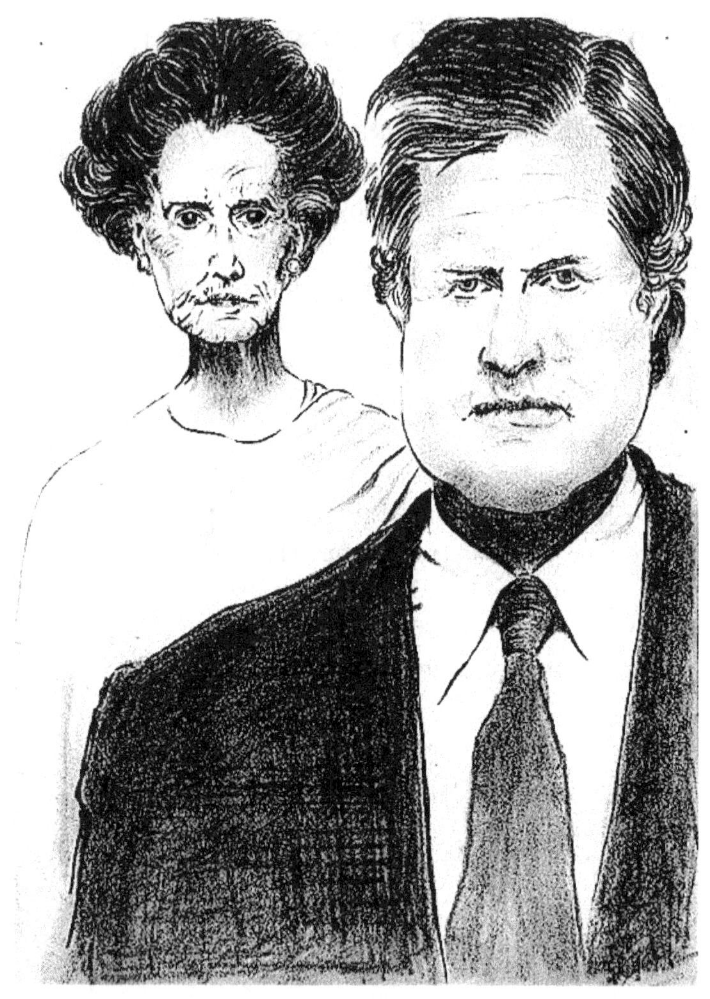

'TEDDY & ROSE'
Pencil on Cartridge Paper, 1976

RETRIEVAL FRAGMENT

To sleep within a bog, beneath a cairn ...
the gift of being human, simply man.
But, internment in a hollow log
to rest as some bright totem
and have such friends as they would place
your remnants, borne aloft in grace
as one who shared not in their blood
but shared their brotherhood and love ...

To such degree, accord respect
with your remains, they could bedeck
and bear in sorrow deeply-felt,
within a tree trunk, held aloft ...
embalmed within, inscribed without
in symbolism scribed with pride;
in language of an ancient race
forever more, your soul embrace.

To be so loved, to be a part
of people's dreaming sacred heart ...
This world should hold like reverence
for superficial difference
where sameness lives beneath all skins
and all blood flows from common springs.

(Some thoughts, following a sensitive documentary on the burial
of a white helicopter pilot, dear, through his friendship and service,
to an aboriginal community in The Gulf Country of Australia.)

REVISITING'S A TURNING
IN THE MIND

Revisiting's a turning in the mind
to regions where mind ought not wish to go ...
to pace again those paths akin in kind
to patterns we should in good sense, now know.
Returning to the space which we once left ...
repeating of the patterns we once knew
is not designed to heal a soul bereft
 nor lead us from a place we should eschew.

Re-written scripts replace the tapes we score ...
the moment moves on at an unseen pace,
brings comprehension we cannot ignore
in seeking out our own small point of grace.
Revisited's another time's tabloid ...
read it with care or otherwise avoid.

(A Shakespearean sonnet)

DUSK HAIKU

My dog fleas herself
In time to frog serenades ...
Dusk on a spring day.

FOR MAURIE ... 15 OCTOBER 2006

A gentle soul once gently filled this space,
Was known by all to some or more degree ...
Too late perhaps, we recognise his grace.

Bookshelf to bar and back, each day his pace
Belied the truth that few might truly see ...
A gentle soul once gently filled this space.

Too often kindness has an unseen face,
Consideration looks for no decree ...
Too late perhaps, we recognise his grace.

Though scorned or loved, some truths cannot efface
The truth that lived and loved for all to see ...
A gentle soul once gently filled this space.

So now he's gone and empty seems this place
He occupied so quietly and free ...
Too late perhaps, we recognise his grace.

It's often when one's gone without a trace,
We yearn to know the depths we did not see ...
A gentle soul once gently filled this space;
Too late perhaps, we recognise his grace.

(A villanelle)

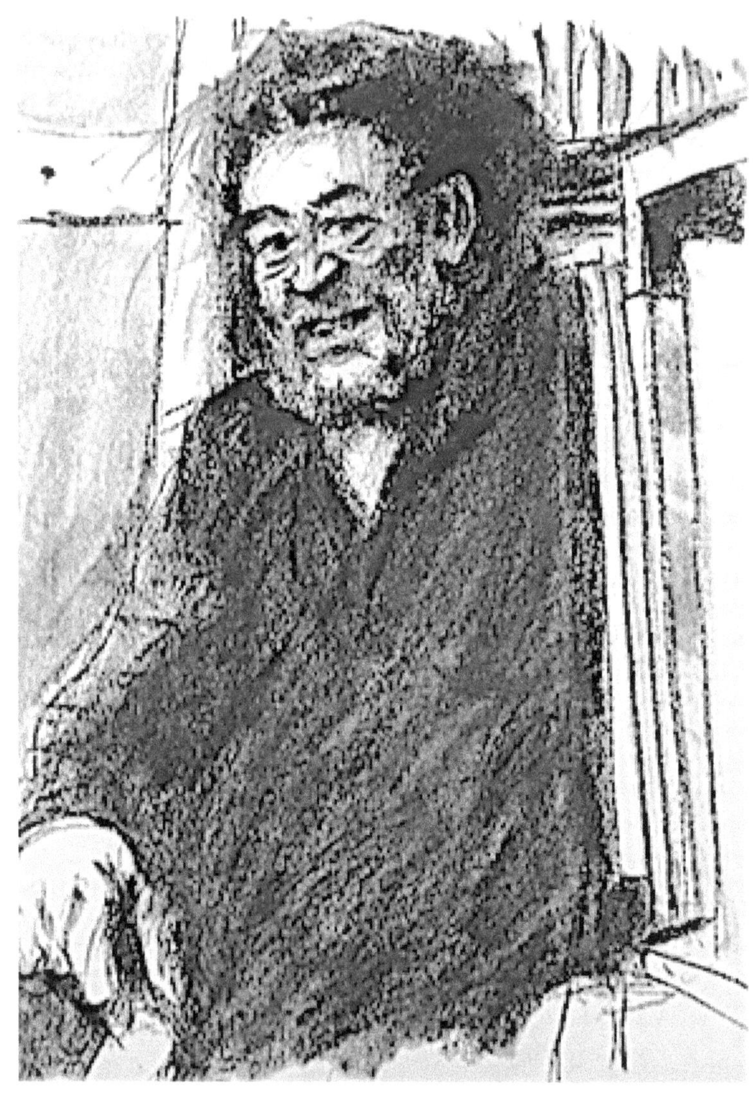

'MAURIE'
Conte crayon on Fabriano Paper, 2015

HOW DEFTLY RUN

How deftly run
the ruminations of a twilight ...
Locked as twilights do,
between the margins of two worlds.

Greens flush the day's last rush
as hollows deepen, shadows lengthen ...
Soft ambers overwhelm these hills
as late glows fade to autumn twilight

And greys of evening slip the day
to cloak the path to midnight ...
All colours soften on the road
through sundown and beyond.

HAIKU ON RISING

Sunbeam through cloud-banks ...
Which is it to be today,
My autumn hilltop?

THE DAY AFTER HAIKU

Steady grey daybreak ...
Distant spatters on rooftops
Talk of her absence.

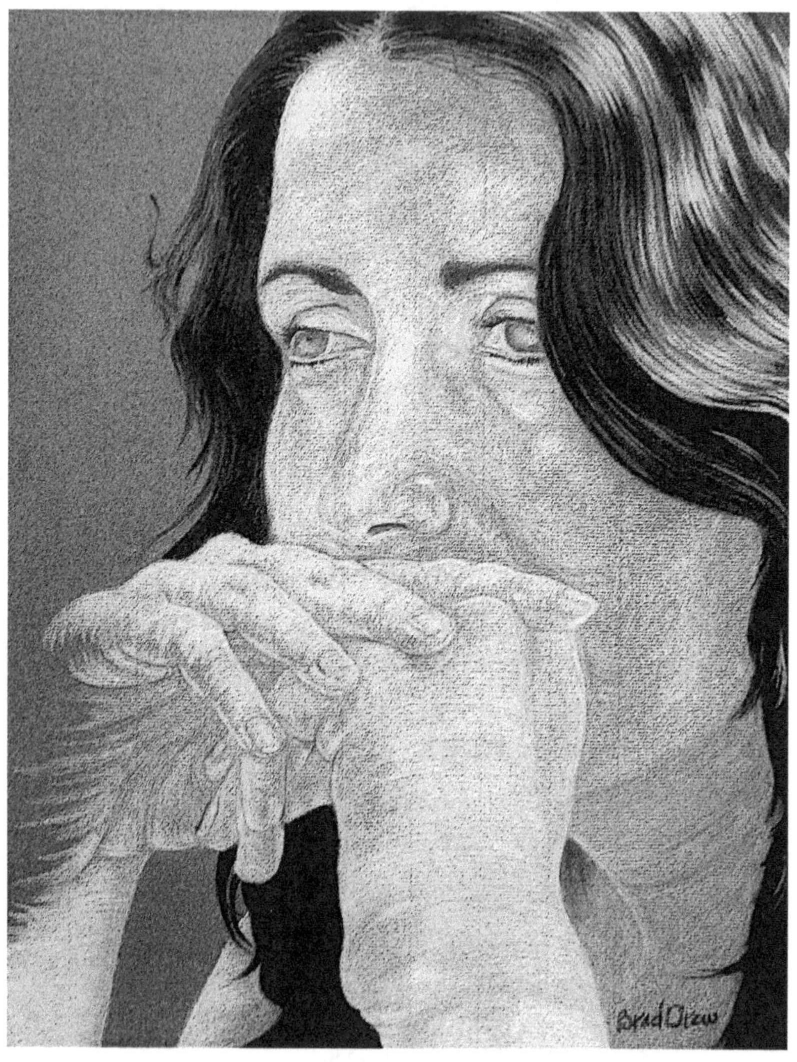

'MAURINE'
Coloured pencil on tinted Ingres Paper, 1974
(From the coloured original)

HOW CAME WE TO THIS DARKNESS?

How came we to the darkness of this place again?
How leisurely the seams do fall apart
and frayed threads lose their grip on all that's bright ...
For bright you were; twice-met it seems ... or more?

How swiftly-spent, the margins of the self do blur;
do shift the threads that bind them, shift and fade.
The carousel will turn, another blur descend the stair ...
A frozen moment played out for all time.

And so to grief again we turn
in sorrow's loss, the past to burn ...
but what should past become once more the now;
encounter dragons we had thought long-slain;
to find the dream, long-lost and spent ...
The present, one more stain?

How came we to the stillness of this place once more?
This instant's keening, lost again to time ...
one moment's keening song, the past to chide;
all efforts at a present, fresh, deride.

And swiftly-gone, the heartbreaks
and the loves long-spent;
infinity's swift instant, evermore ...
For some, life is a moment from the past, replayed.
The carnival's mad frenzy writes the score.

A FENG SHUI CLEARING

Last season's lillypilly
had overhung and overgrown
my 'relationships corner'
and leaf mulch covered its heart ...
fat dark worms had prospered
whilst one white lazy centipede,
assuming kingship of the dank and dark,
presided in sloth-like majesty ...
And over all, hung the heavy stench
of feline dung deposited
by next-door's newfound cat.

Yesterday
in early-winter optimism ...
strange time of year for this
I must admit ... but then,
admissions have become an easy thing ...
and if not now, then when?
So, yesterday I pruned and raked ...
opened up a corner in my heart;
let in the light of optimism and intent;
cleared the ground and aired the earth.

And today? ...
symbolically, I've cleared the path
and freed the gate, built upon
its two-fold purpose ...
invited in fresh love.
Tomorrow, I'll add lights
set to show the way at night ...
for whom? I've no idea ...
Perhaps it's just for me.

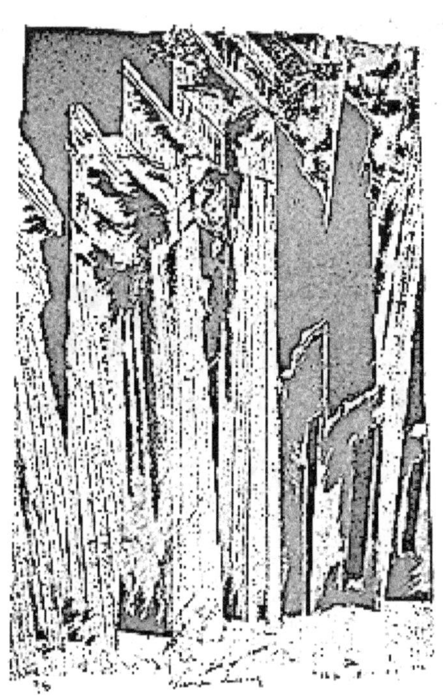

'ATHENIAN WIND HARP'
Screenprint on Arches Dessin Paper, 1983
(From the full-colour original)

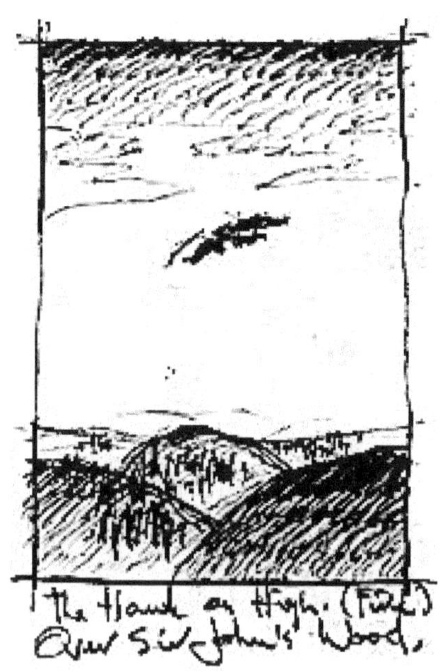

OVER SIR JOHN'S WOOD'
Pencil study for screen print, 1980

TWIN EAGLES RISE

Twin eagles rise through half-light skies;
chase late November's sullen afternoon
to drop, bank, soar ... to sweep and rise again;
grace dusk-stained embers of this fading day
with winds just right to bear the might
of wedge-tailed majesty ... and death.

Death on a rising updraft glides
and soars above the last-light valley ...
last for one whose end has come ...
mute benediction, signed in stealth
and shifting shadows in the blush,
last flush of gold and crimson on the hills.

Death down the spiralling updraft slides,
drawn through the five-hued talons of his eyes
to the prey who waits him, calls him down,
tolled by the knell the cattle wear ...
at forest edge, on hillock's last illumined rise,
sudden and unseen, drops death.

The hill falls still, as homeward-cattle-bound
peal out the ending of another day, and life;
a lowing hymn marks out their hoof-steps,
deep and mild. Light fades ...
the updrafts falter and are gone ...
gone too, the pinioned majesties of air.

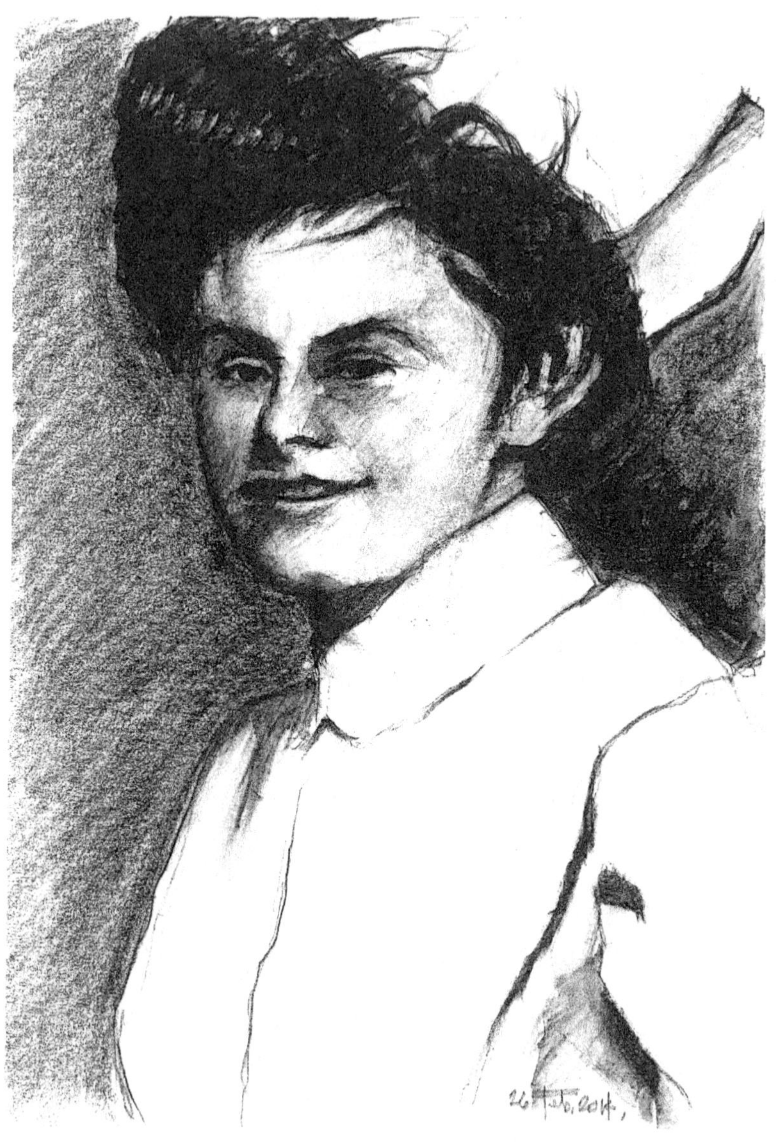

'DOROTHY THOROGOOD, DURING WW2'
Aquarelle graphite pencil & wash on Cartridge Paper, 2014

SONG FOR A FLAT WORLD

They told me that the world be flat;
that there be dragons
and after them, be monsters.
Venture past a certain point ...
all else will fall away.

Yet, like reborn Columbus,
I've set my sails and headed east ...
one compass bearing, all I need –
some landfall ... and the promise
of the sought-for new world calls.

Fair such skies as beckon, lead
into the grail-lit morning;
and fair the song the trade winds sing
so softly, through our rigging;
and fair, the course that's set;

and fair, the seas to follow ...
some landfall on a promised shore
beyond the flat-edge world.
Dare to venture past this point ...
all else will fall away.

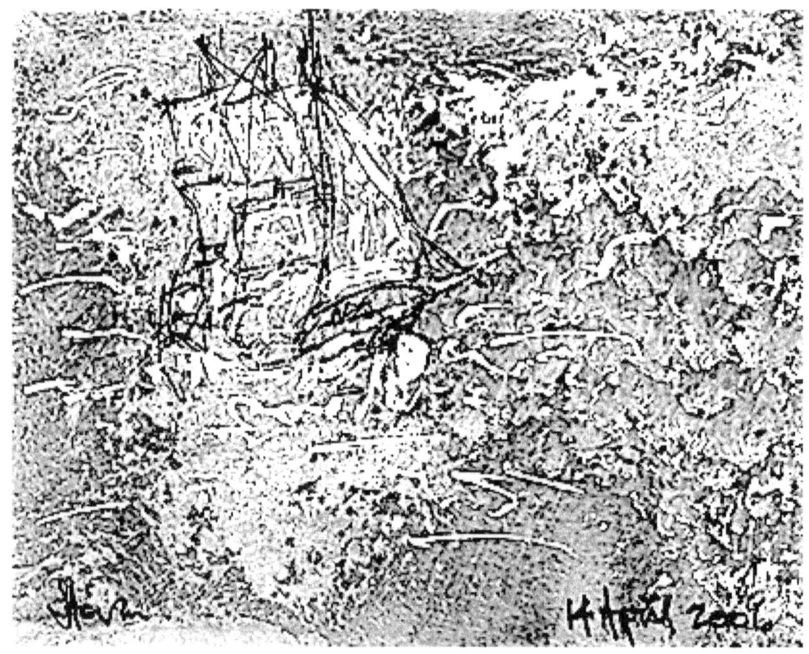

'SHIP IN STORM'
Rollerball & whiteout on rusted Arches Paper, 2006

YET ANOTHER SONG OF SONGS :
'Oh my Beloved, my Song of Songs, and you, the Songstress ...'

CANTO I

Hearken, oh my Love, for I bear no falseness in my words,
   nor with flattery beguile;
   and I know, am well-aware in truth, the timing of our years.
Nor do I speak from kindness, nor in mute consideration –
   this is my Song of Songs
   and is in truth, my sole account of thee ...
Not through rose glasses I, but rather, what my heart knows
   of thee; and what I see, hear, taste, touch, and smell –
   for I am well-pleased, and humbled, and beset by thee.

My Love, you are comely, fair and full with love and joy;
   you are wisdom and mystery to me –
   good sense and soft enigma.
Tender, and terrible of influence, you pervade
   and navigate my sleep;
   drain me of sound reason –
I am lost and helpless before thee
   and I know no more ... no, naught ...
   of life before you entered.

My Love, you are my skin, my joy, my fear
    and daily, the thought of you
    haunts my every moment.
You are my life, my inner substance,
    my suspended sentence
    and my welcome cause.
I could not, would not,
    cage your freedom song
    nor rob thee of its content.

And oh, my Love, my heart delights most
    in your glance
    and your smile lights up my being.
You are my raison d'etre; and my heart would ever chase you,
    sans raison ...
    for you are my night and day, my moon and sun,
My every breath of being ... I am eclipsed,
    and I discover
    I am incomplete without thee.

My Love, my Heart, you inhabit my dreams and strew my paths
    with the leaves and litter of longing, while my heart groans
    and breaks, before and upon each parting ...
Thus likewise, sighs and leaps my heart upon each meeting
    and I am ever well-favoured;
    and so amply-blessed.
You mark the measures of my sleep and dreams
    and magnify my green and clumsy foolishness;
    in foolishness, I say too much ... too much I fear, of me ...
    and ask too much of thee.

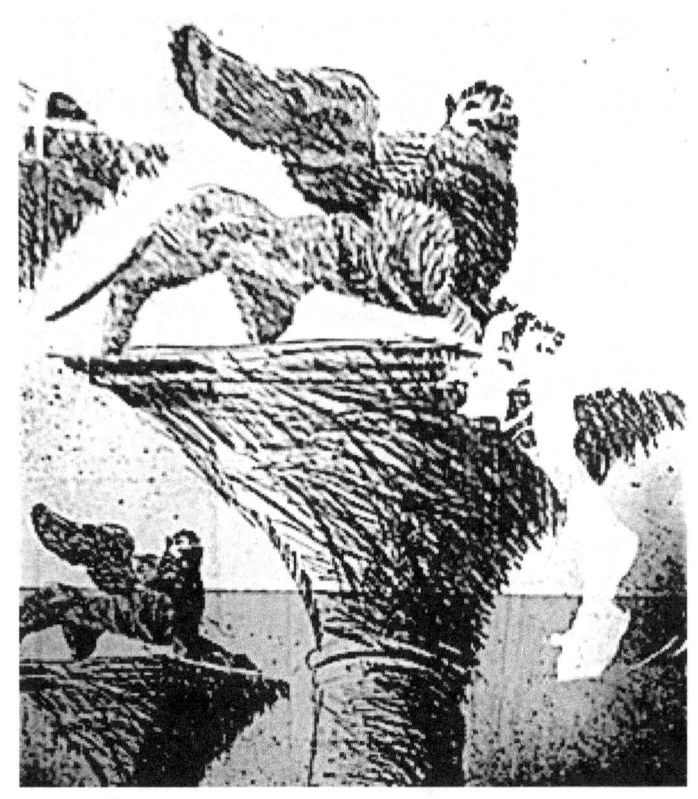

'LIONS OF ST MARK'S, VENICE'
Pencil & ink on Tracing Film, 1983

CANTO II

It is autumn, oh my Love. Our years are numbered –
the month is April...
and July is distant still.
Autumnal bloom enfolds you (as wish I might, would I);
and you are sweet;
and filled with sugars of the season.
Your skin is soft and velvet with all fullness
of the season's bloom, fragrant and enticing;
and I cherish the linger of its smell, held
in linen of the bed and bath, you leave behind thee.

Your breath is sweet, your kiss elusive; I pursue them
both, with ardency and sweet desire... I chase them
like some shy doe, for a single moment's touch.
Your touch thrills me and delights;
gentle and tender;
your fingers are soft and loving.
You are all gentle shyness of the forest doe, my Love:
and I would not chase thee down nor cage thee...
rather, tend your needs, nourish and protect thee.

Look upon me, oh my Love and smile that I might see
the loving favour in thine eyes; for thine eyes
are two soft pools over the gentle fervour of thy heart.
Look upon me, oh my Love and smile that I might taste
the fullness of thy lips; for thy lips are soft,
generous and breathe the air of love.
Your breath and love are soft and sweet;
precious as rare oils and spices... breathe into me
your essence and the incense of thy love.

Show only to me, your morning and your evening face
    in all its purity and freshness...
    for it is the face I most treasure and adore.
Show only to me, your private face, the first and last
    of each day's wearing... for it is your most lovely,
    fresh and youthful face
    and wears the cleanness of your love.
I see your morning, evening, private face, oh my Love,
    with all the jealousy of a lover...
    mine alone to cherish and I would not share its beauty.

Hold me and enfold me, oh my Love,
    store me in your secret places
    and lay me up for winter, should it ever come...
And I will be warm coals to ease your chill;
    my arm, a safe place and a pillow, for your head;
    my body's curve, thy shelter from the wind.
It is autumn, my Love... thy season's bloom is greater
    than the months and years that fed it; I would store it
    in the safe place of my heart,
    when winter winds might blow.

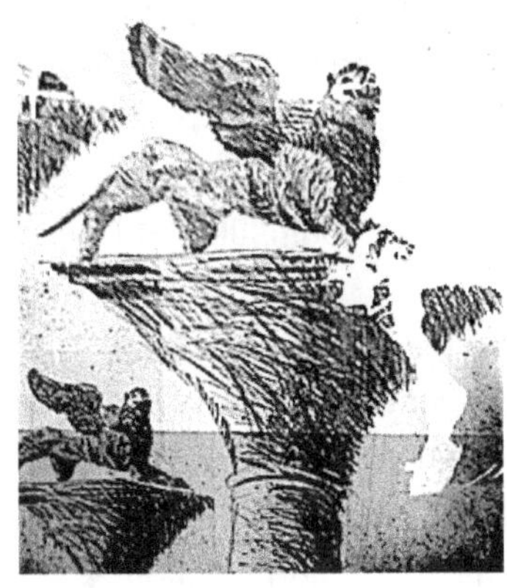

CANTO III

I watched for my Beloved, twenty-thousand nights;
   waited on her, called upon her name
   which none did know...
And searched I every lane, outpost
   and byway for her sign.

And lo, I followed and pursued her shadow
   down the byways and backwaters of my life
   to no avail and no effect.
So many times mistook another for her,
   started at a promise, unfulfilled and incomplete.

I asked in turn, 'Are you she for whom
   my soul does hunger and does yearn...
   are you my heart's great longing and desire?'
And she said, 'Maybe'... or 'No, but I will stay awhile
   to comfort thee... but nothing more.'

I thought I saw her once and chased her shadow;
   chased and lost, then chased again...
   each time the shadow lengthened
And my heart lost heart and closed upon itself
   for still the name which none did know.

Where are you, my Loved and Longed-for One
   in whom I do believe and trust
   and where do you reside
   these twenty-thousand nights
I've waited for you, called your name,
   the name which none do know?

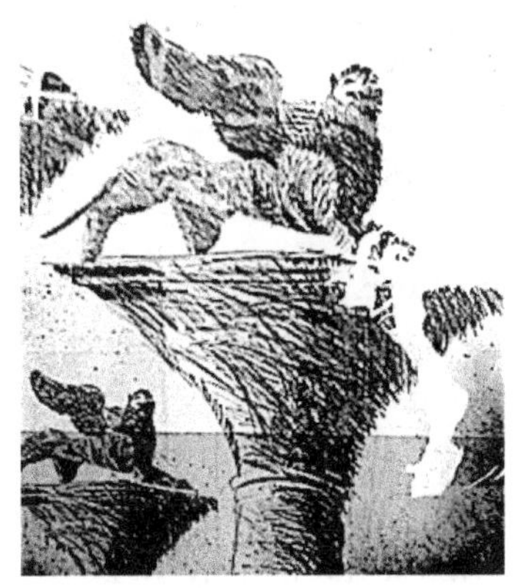

CANTO IV

Hearken, oh my Love, for you are comely
    and more than passing-fair to me; though I know
    full-well the truth in timing of our years.
Oh, you are spring in autumn
    and I would follow thee with faith
    beyond the end of days.
Your eyes are two soft and gentle pools
    where drowns my heart; with cheeks and lips
    lush with the bounty of the season's ripeness.

I would taste the fullness of your lips
    and draw into me
    the sweetness of your breath;
For your lips are soft and your speech is sweet.
    Your voice is a balm unto my ears
    and your song, the transport of my heart.
I would hear thy voice
    and hold it to my soul
    when all else fades, is gone.

Speak to me, my Love,
    that I might know your heart
    and hearken to its call.
Speak to me,
    that I might hear your voice
    and mark its music through my soul;
For thy speech is a sweet
    and gentle balm
    which holds me in its thrall.

Behold and listen ...
    the lark who thrills the glade
    fills and binds the soul.
Sing with me, my Love,
    draw near to me
    and sing the balance of our days...
For you are a lark unto my life,
    evensong and vespers
    for my timely day.

Hearken, oh my Love, for you are comely
    and your voice,
    the joy of lark-song fair to me;
Your eyes, two pools to plunge
    and lips to breathe and taste,
    full transport for my soul;
Your breath as sweet as speech...
    the spikenard and balm
    to soothe my days.

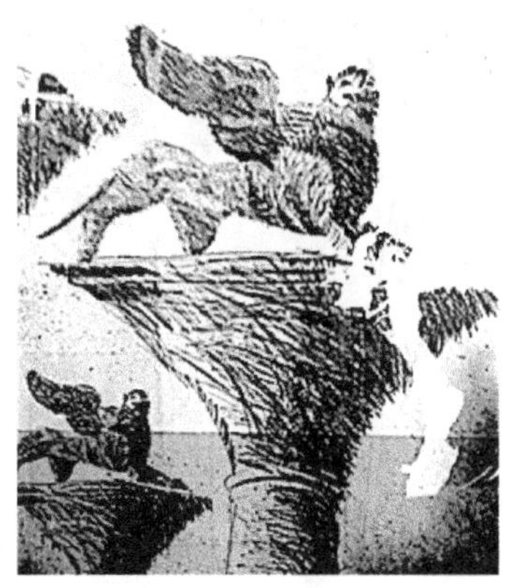

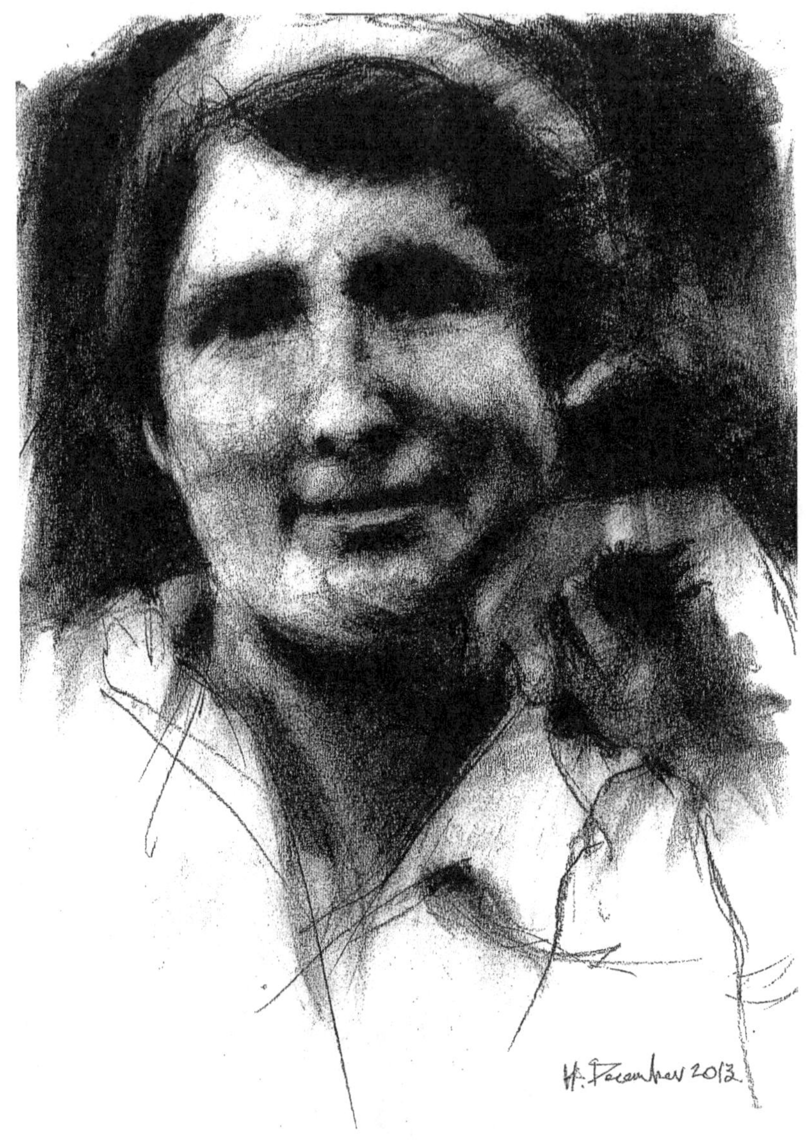

'MY GREAT AUNT, EFFIE HIGGENSON, AS A YOUNG WOMAN'
Conte crayon on Cartridge Paper, 2013

CANTO V

I glimpsed her, then I found her,
    she whose name none ever knew.
And I drew her to me
    that I might better see her face.
There, loveliness resides and has my heart
    overtaken and undone.
And my heart leaps to her, sings in joy
    then cries out in her absence.
Her name is Softness and Beauty
    and I am forever lost.

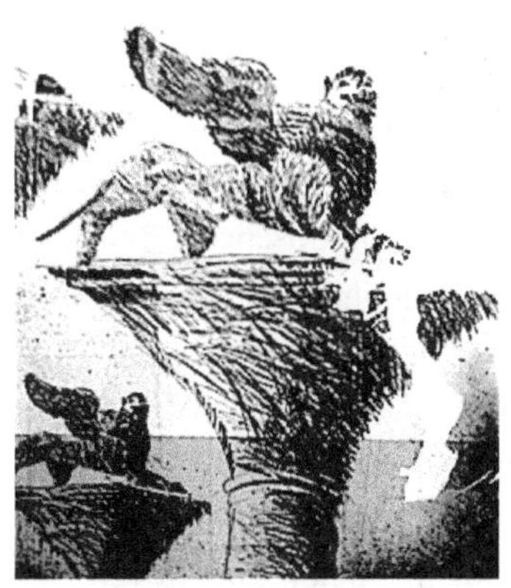

CANTO VI

Beloved mine, you are all tenderness at once
    and terrible... all terrible as an army
    that lays siege and sacks my nights;
For sleep as I might, my heart does wake me
    to the drumroll of thy absence
    and my un-slept longing knows no bounds.

Your image, person and your voice
    draw me from sleep and I am beset
    by the banners and the marching of your host.
You walk among my dreams, my Love,
    soft-shod and urgent
    and thy quiet footstep stirs my unquiet night.

Beloved mine, you tend the garden of my being;
    its beds are full to overflowing with the bounty
    of your fruit and blossoms.
You are the bee who tends, for you fertilise
    and feed my hunger; yet steal my appetite,
    shore up my zest for eating.

Come to me, my Love, and lie with me;
    lay off your siege and let your soft-shod footsteps
    pause and rest spoon-wise in mine.
Let the fullness of your autumn fruit
    quench my thirsting mouth
    and quell my always hunger for thee.

Scatter your blossoms on my brow,
    oh sweetest Love, breathe your sleep
    and slumbering heart with mine...
In the rising and the falling of our breasts
    decamp your army, cease your siege
    and set the standard of your tenderness upon me.

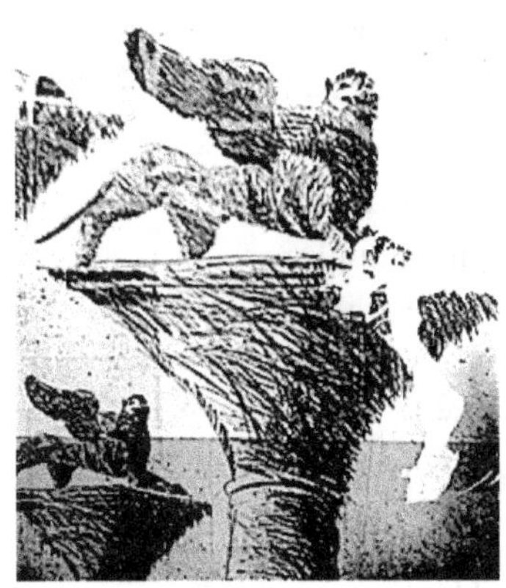

CANTO VII

How beautiful you are, my Love;
    for you are more than passing fair
    and comely in your bearing.
Your very being and your body
    are a well-matched
    and fitting slipper unto mine...
We do wear each other like fitting and
    well-tailored garments, cut and fashioned
    for all seasons and all weathers.
You are beauty, my Love,
    and you bring me to my knees,
    tear my heart asunder.

Your head is a chalice of goodness
    crowned with wisdom.
Your head is a fine and delicate globe
    wreathed by the wildness of your hair,
    a tangle of sacred and profane delights...
Your hair is a joy to me
    and your nose is fine and stately;
    in breath, so soft and sweet.
Your cheeks are high and rounded
    set with smiling dimples
    as ripe pomegranates.

Your eyes are deep with kindness
    and are two pools
    in which I sink to drown.
Your lips are generous
    and I would breathe the honey
    of your lips and tongue.

Your feet are small and eloquent
    and I would kiss and swallow them
    like words of love.
Your calves and thighs are slender saplings
    and your buttocks,
    small and firm as apples.

Your navel is a jewelled thimble
    set in the gentle swell ...
    a small boat moored upon a gentle sea.
The gentle swelling of your belly
    is a soft basket ...
    container of your warmth and goodness.
Your breasts are the bounty of two peaches,
    flowing and full
    with autumn juices...
And you are full with love for me
    and my pulse quickens
    with your warmth.

Oh, my Love of Loves, you fill me with desire,
    hasten my breath
    for my hand is want upon thee.
Your name is Softness and Beauty,
    Quickness and Desire...
    and I would fain lie with you
    to be thy grist and core.
Would that I could breathe your breath
    and share the beating of your heart.
    Lock me within thee, oh my Love,
    and never let me go ...
For I am yours alone;
    I am your troth and would
    that thou were truly pleased with me.

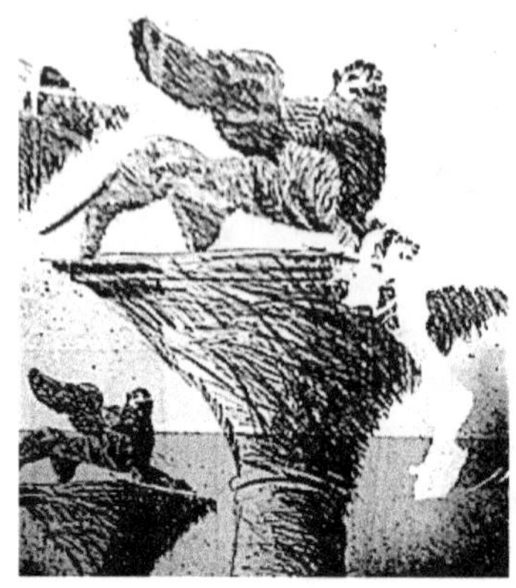

CANTO VIII

Hurry, oh my Love, and squeeze out
   the fullness of each moment
For I am your Love and have waited on you,
   called your name,
     these twenty-thousand nights...
And your name is Lovely, Beauty,
   Softness and Desire,
     and I am full, well-full, of thee.

Your name, which none could name,
   has marked me
     and is a seal upon my heart.
Your flame ignites my veins
   and will not let me rest
     for you are lovely and do blind my sight.
All I am and would be,
   is in thee, my Love
     and you are my purpose and delight.

Come and twine with me, my Love;
    encompass me, hold me close,
    and spill the juices of our season ...
For I will drink your heady wine,
    anoint you
    with the nectar of my being;
And I will cradle thee from the storm,
    my arm a pillow
    and a comfort to thy soul.

Speak to me, my Love, and call my name
    as I've called yours
    and shout, for all the world to hear.
Take my hand and clasp it to your heart,
    pull my arms about you;
    swallow my mouth and drown me in your fire,
For I am mad-crazy for you
    and would have thee melt for me.

Clasp my hand and walk with me, my Love,
    and wear each moment in your breast...
For I would fain share
    and hold each moment with you,
    adore you to the end.
You are contentment and great joy to me,
    oh my Love... my reason
    and the absence of all reason.

(With respectful apologies
to one 'Solomon, King'.)

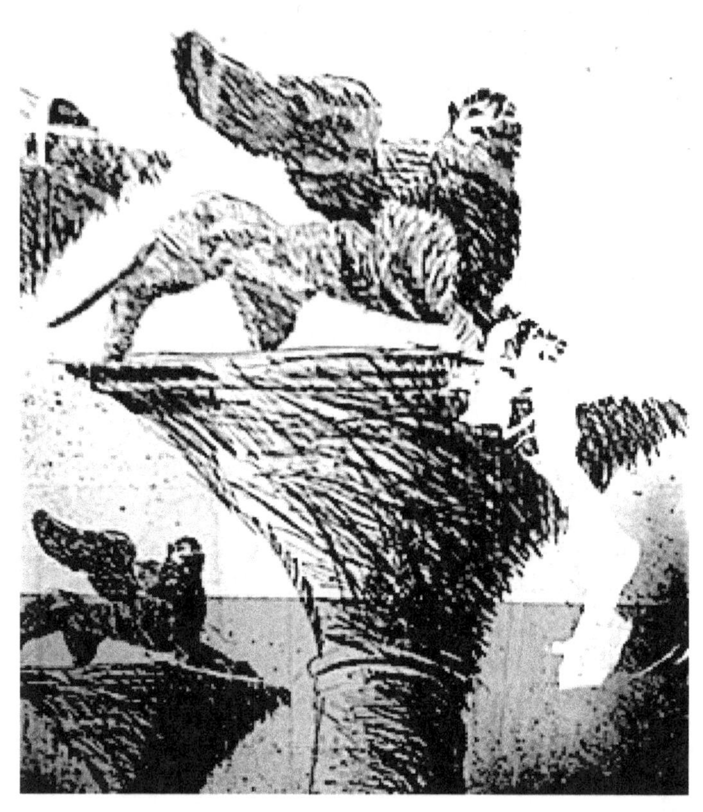

'LIONS OF ST MARK'S'
Pencil & ink on Tracing Film, 1983

YOU ARE MY SONG

You are my evening and my autumn song
and you would be the last I'd wish to sing;
as autumn moves to winter, short or long –
I'll sing you still, whatever time may bring.
I'll sing your song with passion and with joy,
with tenderness and sweet gentility –
and if time's passage should that voice destroy,
your melody will linger clear and free.

Should you consent to hold me and my love
against your heart and ear for all of time,
your song, your name, will charge my heart above
all others and to yours, my voice will climb.
For you remain my substance, my delight –
you are the song that fills me, day and night.

(A Shakespearean sonnet)

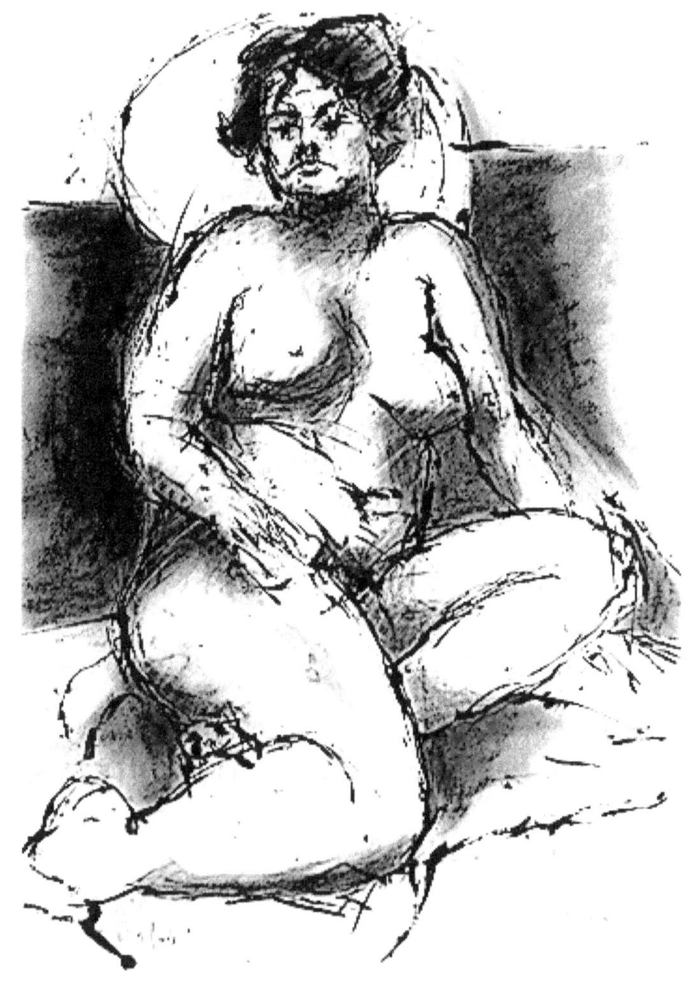

'SEATED WOMAN'
Sharpened stick, ink & charcoal on Cartridge Paper, 2009

I THINK YOU HAVE, MY HEAD UNDONE

I think you have, my head undone;
by all that's light and all that's bright
I know, my heart, you've overrun –

for as your landfall hove in sight
you furled my sails some twelve months past
with all your light, by all that's bright.

Though fly our days and seasons fast,
moored in these new world's waters sound,
you've furled my sails these twelve months past.

Much goodness in your soul resounds
and in your presence, I am blessed –
moored in these waters, safe and sound.

I know you have, my heart possessed;
yours is the grail that brings me light
and by your presence I am blessed.

You show me beauty as my right;
I feel you have, my past undone.
Yours is the grail that lights my night –
I know, my heart, you've overrun.

(A terzanelle, derived from the villanelle and terza rima forms)

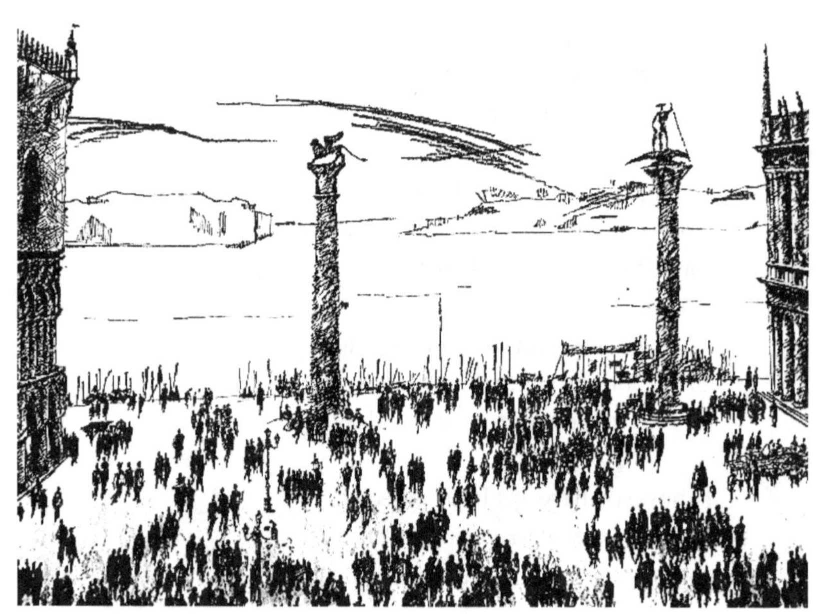

'ST MARK'S SQUARE' Detail
Rapidograph on Tracing Paper, 1983

UPON THE NEW WORLD LANDFALL

A safe and pleasant mooring, sheltered and abundant;
Furled the sails and anchored deep
The sirens' song lost to their sleep ...
Our ship rides gently on the swell of harboured rest
And all around, our new world's charms attest
The rightness of our landfall.

At harbour's edge, so spreads our landfall verdant ...
This promised shore, this haven, keep;
Both Eden and a place to reap
The harvest of a journey started long years past
When different helmsmen stood before the mast
To hold us each in thrall.

For you alone, are journey's end ...
Your verdant country, I will tend
With love and dedication;
Our damaged paths and fields to mend;
Along your ways I'll gladly wend
With easy step, forsaking hesitation.

A POEM FOR VALENTINE

The season's February and Cupid's come
in winged haste, all quiver and bow ...
Summer wanes through her last glow.

Hart, hare and hound retreat, as kite
soars high to cry the season's exit
to Autumn and the Fall ...

As once did Psyche's sisters fall,
Eros-lured, in other times
and half a world full-distant.

In our own Autumn, Spring revives again;
entreats both wary and the not-so,
to once again be mine and share
the sweetness of this arrow drawn.

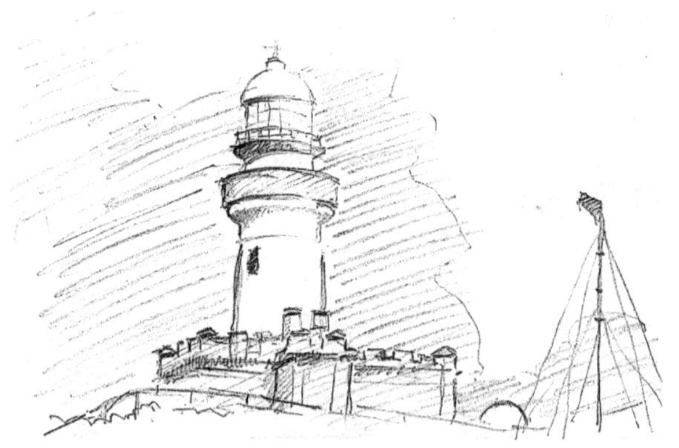

'LIGHTHOUSE, BYRON BAY'
Notebook pencil sketch, 1979

THREE YEARS OUT

Three years from landfall on that promised shore
when hearts were light and buoyant to the cause
while verdant, through the mists, new Eden rose
around us, fresh with lushness and so clean
the air itself glowed with an inner light ...
so came safe harbour, comfort, pure and bright.

No place is free of goblins, nor of ghosts ...
the same proved true for this new world, our host;
for as we staked our claim and marked our plots,
faint ghosts were glimpsed to dart at vision's edge
but as we plumbed and charted out our shore,
discovered shoals and reefs but little more.

We chart our waters carefully, now we know
and watch for where waves break amid safe flows;
look out for goblins in the fairy dells
or ghosts whose whispers break the season's spell;
for true our landfall is and fair our barque ...
this journey's ours ... how could we disembark?

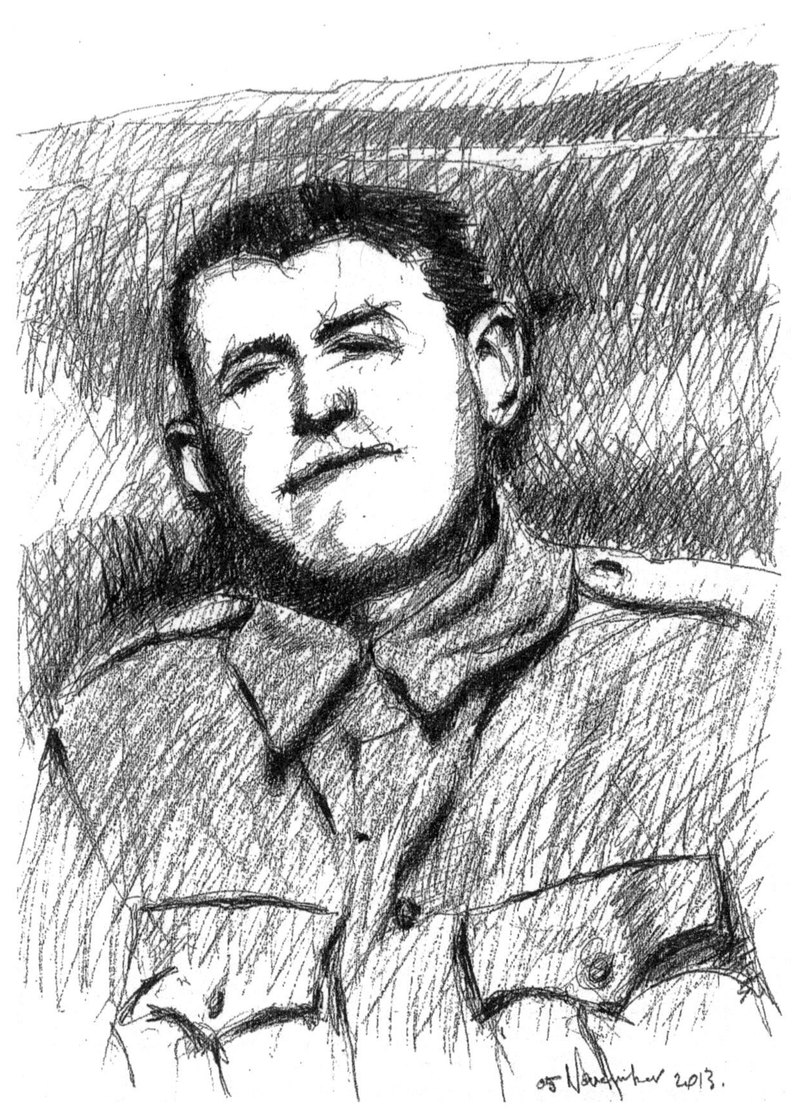

'MY GREAT-UNCLE, ROBERT HIGGENSON IN FLANDERS FIELDS, 1916'
Graphite stick on Cartridge Paper, 2013

A POEM FOR CHRISTMAS

Morning ... and insistent dawn
slips past shutters, dreams and sleep.
I sense your stirring, tuned to mine;
your gentle breathing and I wonder
whether this slow-waking heat is yours
or that of oncoming day?

Yet another solstice done,
days shorten on the path to autumn
and beyond ... it's almost Christmas ...
while the gift you are, warms and heartens;
stirs daily, gratitude for all your presence
through this Autumn of our seasons.

I watch your waking profile
and wonder at my own good fortune;
listen for the first birds' calling
late in this rising heat of day ...
savour this season and our mountain
to thank the world for whom you are.

AND OF CONTENTMENT ...

I witness summer's winding down
as February sounds her last retreat
and this year's hares still find delight
in dandelions that grace our hill.

All summer, they have come to meet
and sample full, the weeds that crown
our slopes ... dawn brings them here
and dusk returns them still.

No March hare madness this ...
save quiet contentment in
their own familial ways and gentle bliss
as summer greets sweet autumn.

And of contentment, I am mindful
of her easy touch, as all my summers
roll off into one ... the very sum and total
of those which all have come before.

So comes our southern Valentine
lazy with the last of summer's heat
to quietly prompt us all, entreat ...
as I do now ... and ask you to be mine.

FOUR YEARS HAVE COME TO US

Four years have come to us and washed these shores
as varied as the tides, which in their surge
bear mostly treasured shells and little more ...

We've seen our journeys into one converge
despite rare storm-front surges from the past,
as varied as the tides which by us, surge ...

Our voyage, mainly smooth beneath this mast;
astern, the gentle passage of each now,
in spite of storm-front surges from our pasts.

Since setting sail, four years have passed our bow
to run our length and sparkle in our wake
as churns astern, the passing of each now ...

The purpose of this journey's no mistake;
so we must trim our sails and fair seas urge
to run our length and sparkle in our wake ...

For right a voyage is, that would so merge
while years may come to us and wash our shores ...
then, as we trim our sails and fair seas urge,
find mainly pretty shells and little more.

(A terzanelle: derived from the villanelle and terza rima forms)

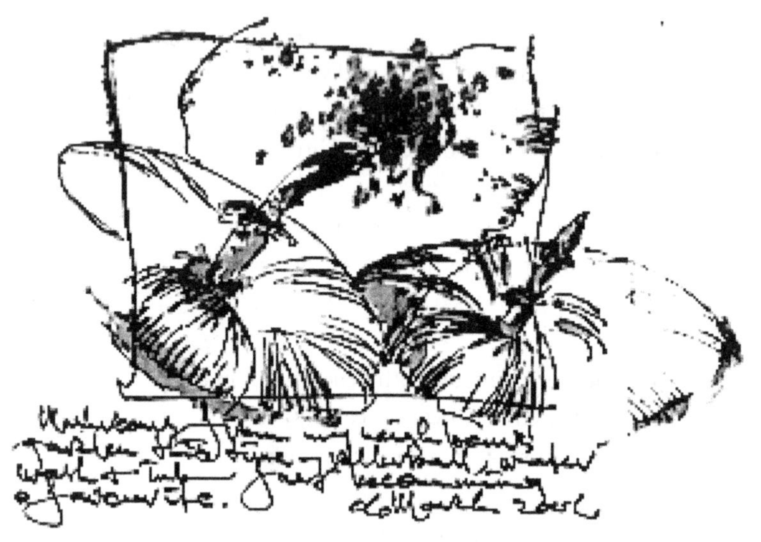

'MUSHROOMS'
Rollerball & wash on Arches Paper, 2006

ONE SEASON'S MOULD

Vinegar! ... And cloves! ...
For weeks it's rained or seems so
as the last of summer's breath lies heavy,
burdens every mote that ever settled
on the contours of my home ...
and spores spring forth in sudden places.

An host is come ...
entrenched its mould-spawned minions;
encamped itself on bulwark and in hollow;
laid siege, established beachheads
on my walls, my couch, my shoes, my belts!
The pungent rotting–citrus bloom springs forth;
adorns them all.

In the village, townsfolk mutter
curse and throng the streets;
storm the shelves of pharmacy and hardware,
both ... for oil of cloves and vinegar;
regroup for bleach in every form ...
as desiccator vendors rub their hands
and dehumidifiers thrum
to drain the hub of humid households.

These then, are the wages
of our mountaintop existence,
lodged along the margins of the clouds;
responding to the fungal fugue
with seasonal insistence,
we air our cupboards, stoke our fires ...
maintain the mushroom vigilance
our treasures to preserve.

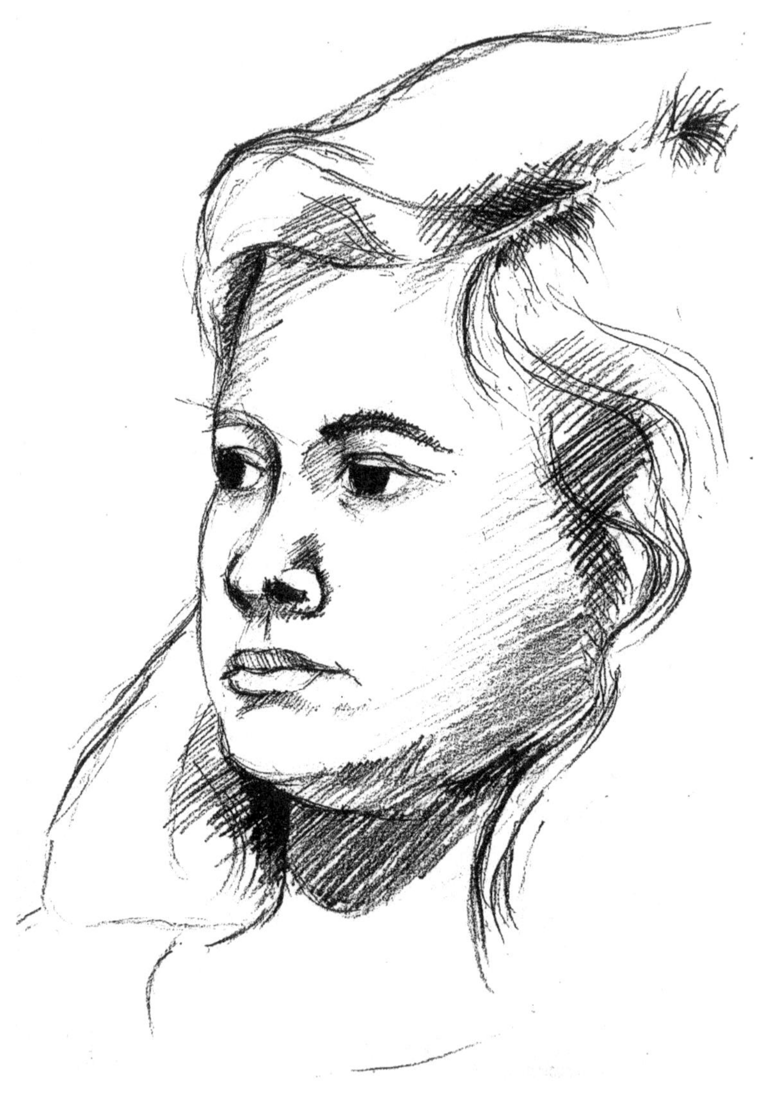

'MY SISTER BRONWYN'
Pencil on Cartridge Paper, 1977

MUTE SUNFLOWERS FROM GREY ASHES

Mute sunflowers from grey ashes sadly rise
their benedictions begging time to stall ...
to see how reason from this world still flies

So brief the time they had to realise
that time could end thus and bright darkness fall
whilst mute, would sunflowers from grey ashes rise

For in that instant stripped of compromise
a final moment from which none might crawl ...
none witness for themselves how reason flies

These scattered parts, confetti of their lives
adorn the landscape ... silence to appall
as mutely sunflowers from sad ashes rise

For while we argue where the true blame lies
news networks vie to hold us in their thrall;
convey how reason from this world now flies

Until another headline sounds its cries
and interests in the current banner pall
mute sunflowers will from ashes, sadly rise
to show how reason from this world still flies.

(A villanelle for The Downing of MH17, 2014)

AS AUTUMN TURNS ...

As autumn turns to sleep with winter's years
and friends recede as hailed by close of day
we seek distractions to allay our fears
that in the end we're little more than clay.
We look for what we might now leave behind
convince ourselves that we might be revered ...
that much of it was not just in our mind
but had a form more valued than was feared.

Spare us from dwelling in a pumped-up past
reliving blown-out visions of our youth;
false vanities devoid of power to last;
mythologies which test the bounds of truth.
Wear old age with such modesty and grace
vain foolishness in old age shan't deface.

(A Shakespearean sonnet)

A SONNET FOR VALENTINE'S

This February has arrived and still
our own fleet hares return to laze and graze
the ever-constant haven of our hill.
Through mists and squall they've come to grace this slope
and brought the young to share these joyous days
which crown their own existence with such hope.

This week has seen them sportive, gay and light;
to leap, spin, turn, cavort across the hill
in mating-mad abandonment's fey flight
to garner all these joys at summer's end;
ward off the threat of hoary winter's chill ...
such is the essence of the path I'd wend
to tarry with you for this little while
and give you some cause, through the mists to smile.

(A terza rima sonnet)

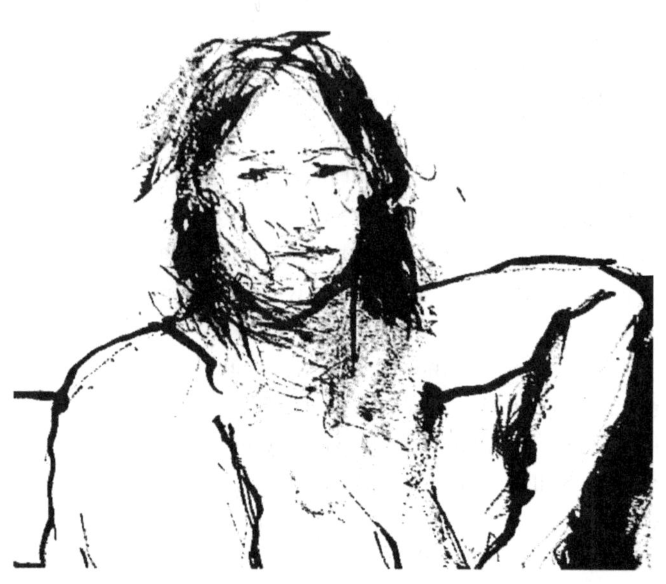

'SEATED WOMAN' Detail
Sharpened stick & Indian ink on Cartridge Paper, 2008

TO LATER FRIENDSHIPS

Friends come and go throughout the flux of life;
they catch the sun to shine and briefly flare
but often, overtaken in life's shade
they find themselves replaced by other cares ...
these mostly not for reasons false or trite
but simply time and distance lets them fade.
Nostalgia meanwhile, holds them in her arms
to hang around our life like chain-linked charms.

And then, there are those others, coming late
as sparks to smoulder in the embers of our day;
who through their strengths will suffer no such fate;
for you my friend will sidestep all the shade
wherein, for time and distance, others laid ...
thus unforgotten, ever shall you stay.

(A variation on the sonnet form)

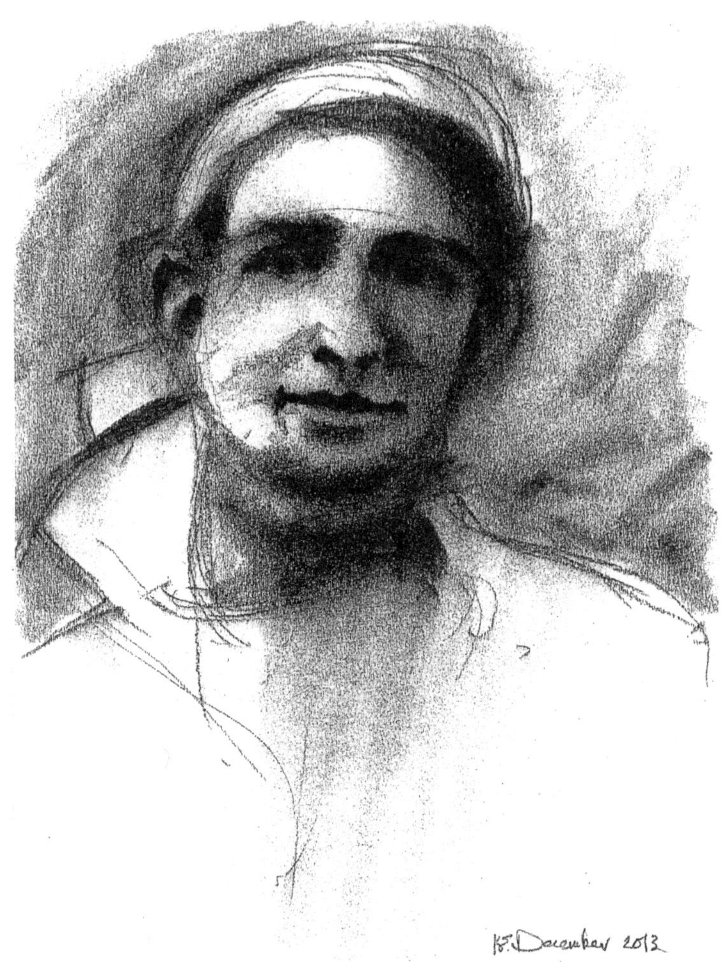

'MY GREAT AUNT, MARY HIGGENSON, IN HER YOUTH'
Conte crayon on Cartridge Paper, 2013

A POEM FOR JULY

At this time of year, I find I've now become
Aware of odysseys and voyages begun
And sailed through latitudes to longitudes uncharted,
As questing eastwards, one reborn Columbus started ...
Sailing far beyond the seas he knew
Through seasons and through climes of changing hue.

When our new Columbus set out for the edge
Of reason or the world he'd come to know;
Or when latter-day Ulysses swore his pledge
To faithfully return at journey's close ...
However might the surge of seas and currents flow
This was the course he so willingly then chose.

Now five years since our odyssey began
And three years since we furled our open sails,
To cast our anchor, settle our new land;
Surmount with love what storm-fronts might assail ...
Thus garner in the harvests of our joy;
Protect our haven and all means deploy
To meld as one, the substance of our lives ...
Plant out our plot, so naught but goodness thrives.

THREE NINDERRY TANKAS

Consigned for all time
Within these stocks, these mute rocks,
Rash Ninderry squats ...
Contemplates eternity
And his ever-present past.

Sitting thus in stocks,
No birds sing for Ninderry ...
Vilified and scorned,
He watches still, the lovers
United by Maroochy's grief.

Still flows the river;
Sheds tears across the flood plain
From range to sea ...
Scattered Coolum finds his rest –
Maroochy's grief, the waves attest.

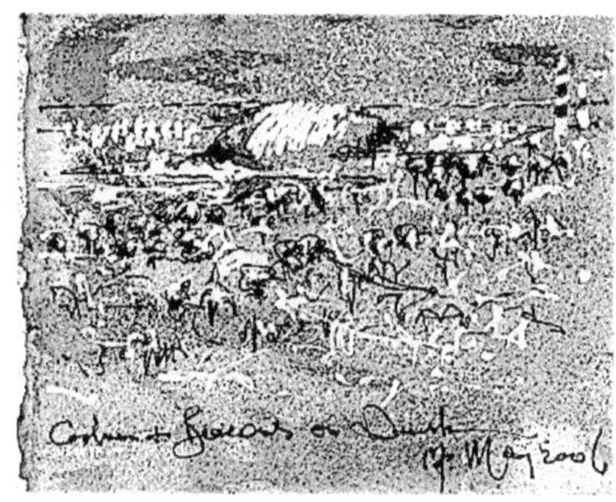

'MT COOLUM & BEACONS'
Rollerball & whiteout on rusted Arches Paper, 2006

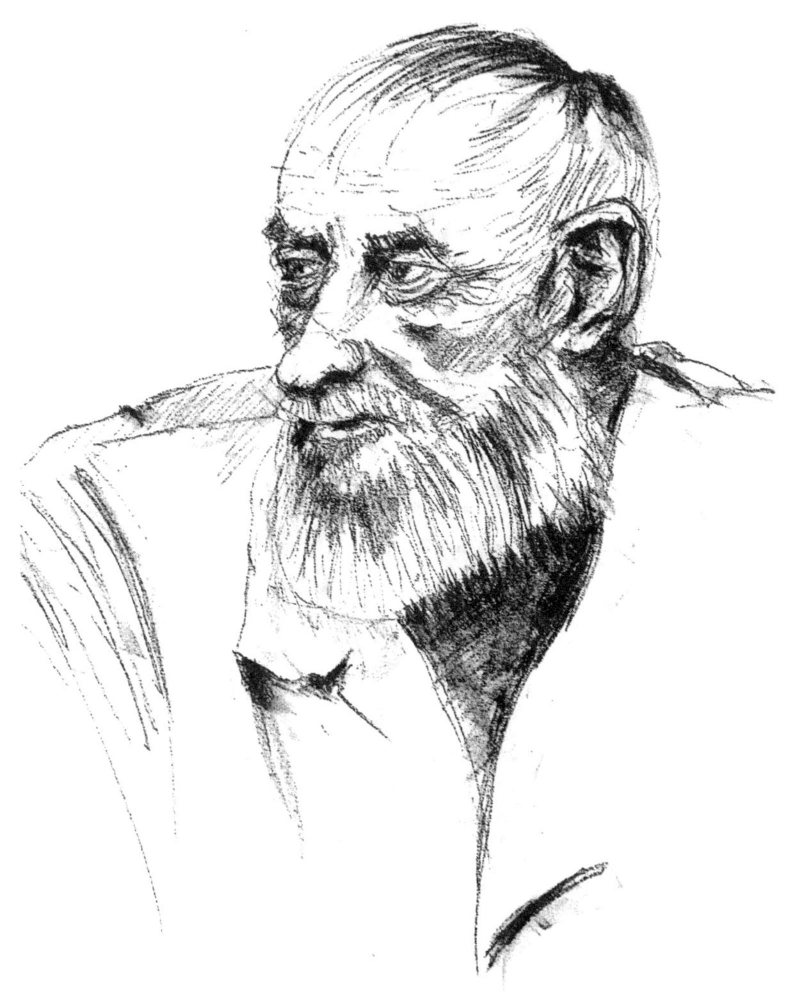

'JIM'
Conte crayon onCartridge Paper, 2008

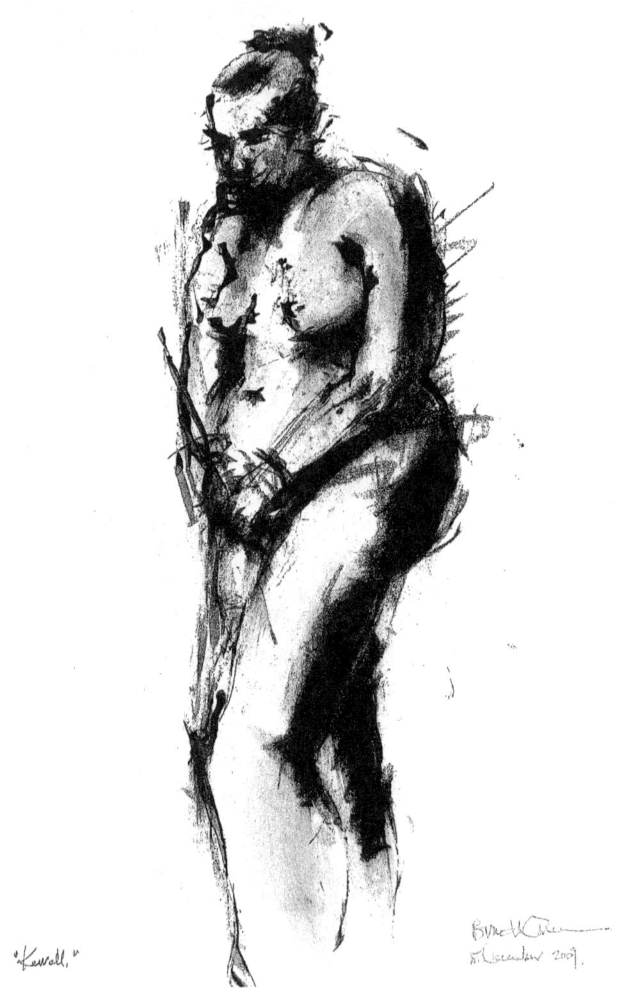

'STANDING WOMAN'
Sharpened stick with Indian ink & charcoal on Cartridge Paper, 2009

BLACKALL RANGE:
THE LATER POEMS
DEC. 2015 TO MAY 2020

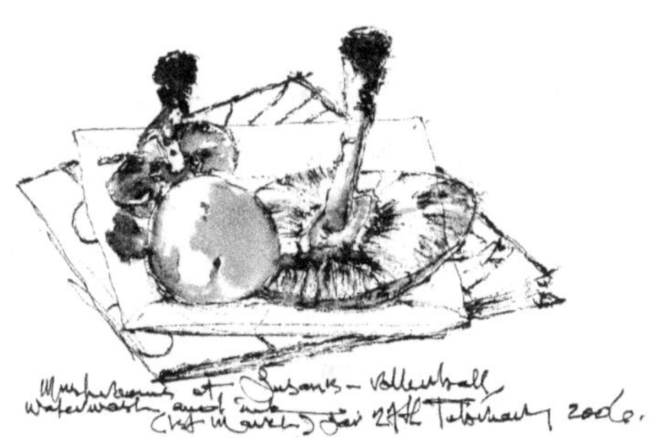

TWO DAYS OUT FROM VALENTINES

Two days out from Valentine's
and not a poem written ...
But still, I ask you to be mine;
There's no questioning, I'm smitten.

This year has come upon us fast.
We never sensed its coming ...
With most things now not meant to last,
we're blessed by love consuming.

As for our hares, they've fled our hill –
moved from our slopes with February's versing.
I guess they've gone ... at least until
we're rid of next-door's barking.

We've written of hart, our hares and hounds –
and kites in the last of summer's light ...
while hounds cry out, no hares will bound,
except through local lanes by night.

While after dusk, they yet may roam;
their memory still lends us hope
that one day soon, they might come home
again once more, to grace our slopes.

We in the meantime, do our best
to make love count above the rest ...
For I am yours; please you, be mine ...
make everyday our Valentine's.

SO HERE WE ARE ...

So here we are and six years out of port
while your life turns about a new decade ...
Who would have dreamed?
Who would have thought
when we safe landfall made,
that freshness at this time of life
could be redeemed?

At water's edge our settlement abounds
upon a delta formed by mergings of two rivers ...
a flood plain rich in silt
twin years have carried down,
to flourish and to grow, in lushness so diverse.

Our vessel rides now safely in our harbour.
The tides lap gently stem to stern, our length
where, deep and clear,
clean waters surge about our anchor ...
Who could have dreamed? Who could believe
what soundness and what strength
that such a New World founded, might conceive?

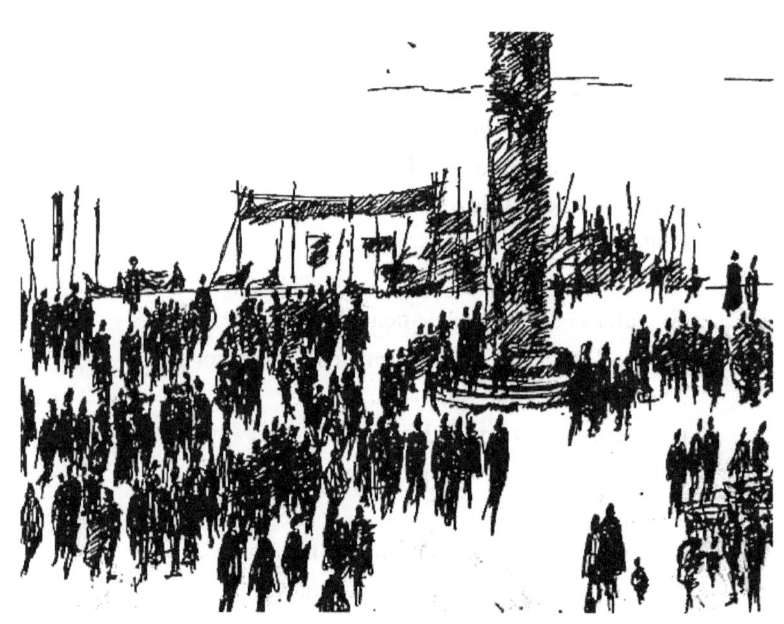

'ST MARK'S SQUARE, VENICE' Detail
Rapidograph on Tracing Paper, 1983

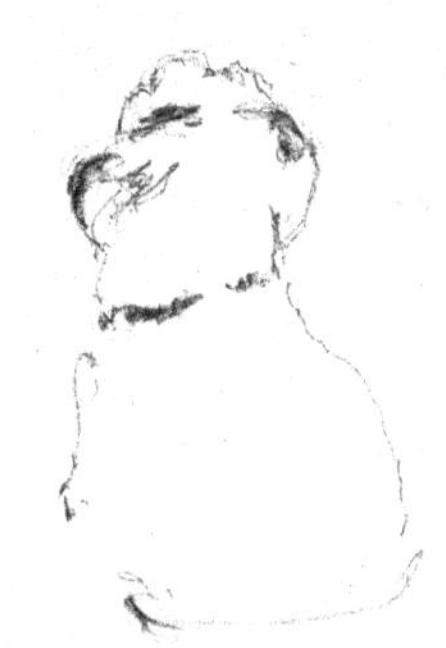

ON DISTANT DOGGY DOTAGE

Seen up this close, each wall becomes a portal
to other worlds ... Reality mislaid.
Frozen in time, he becomes a new Zen master
focused on infinity, while paint films disappear.

Locked in satori's embrace of empty dog-bowl:
watershed of nothingness, beyond all expectation ...
Frozen thus, he'll stand with eye to wall, at thresholds
of infinity in none-ness ... never being there at all.

His days turn on this wheel of life; swinging, where
'eats' and rest form his meridian, guide his bearings;
always to dream ... And dream, he does ...
To sit or stand, soft eyelids drooping –
then full-suddenly to slump ...
Yawn, lick his chops, then slump again.

He perambulates in old man gait, oscillating
between arthritic waddle and pure puppy-manic ...
Walking uphill under heavy load, where a simple shake
sends loose legs scattering ...
Leaves before the Autumn's wind,
sent all cardinal points on one slipped instant ...
Old man locomotion and all traction lost.

Oscillates on soundings of the tea bell ... Reverts
from plodding senior to bright show-pony manic
in one eye's blinking, legs all a-skitter
under the high-borne food bowl ...
To leap and dance high galliards of joy:
anxiety's relief when She-who-must-be-loved
returns to boon some treat.

And thus-rewarded for his patience,
he'll have the last word, with a pee ...
In unexpected places, mostly ... And, stress removed,
drift off to dream enlightenment again.

Perhaps all dotage holds such lands of darkness,
lost in light ... Where eyesight blurs;
where hearing fades; and cunning of the old
lights all such hidden places,
in a twilight of the senses, not all what it might seem ...
Where faux farragoes of decrepitude are bound
to win through, every time.

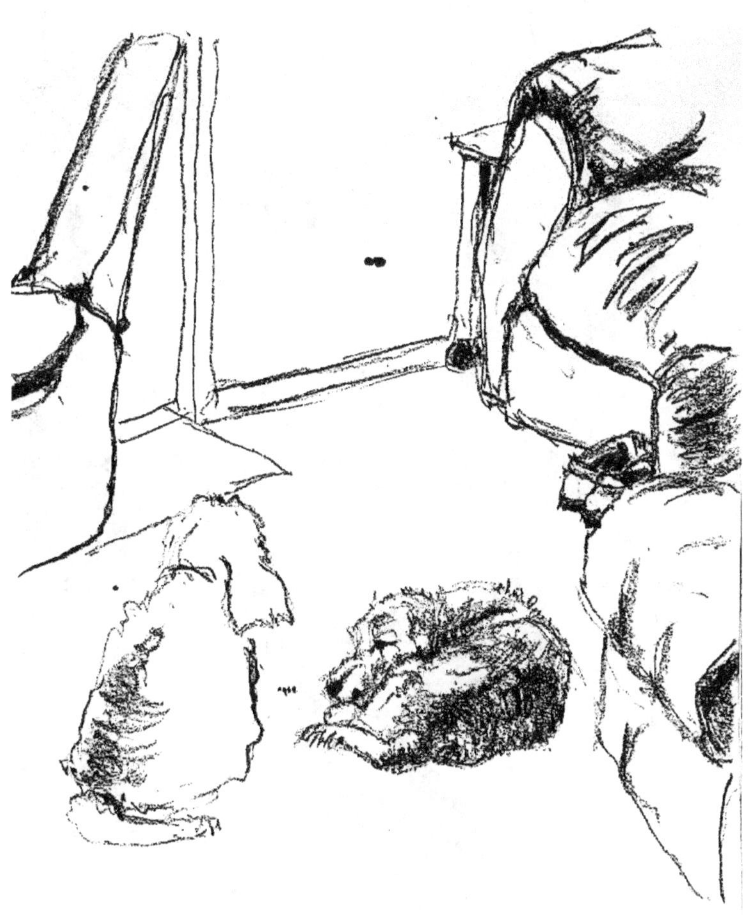

'BENJI', Studies at Hervey Bay.
Charcoal pencil on Cartridge Paper, 2015

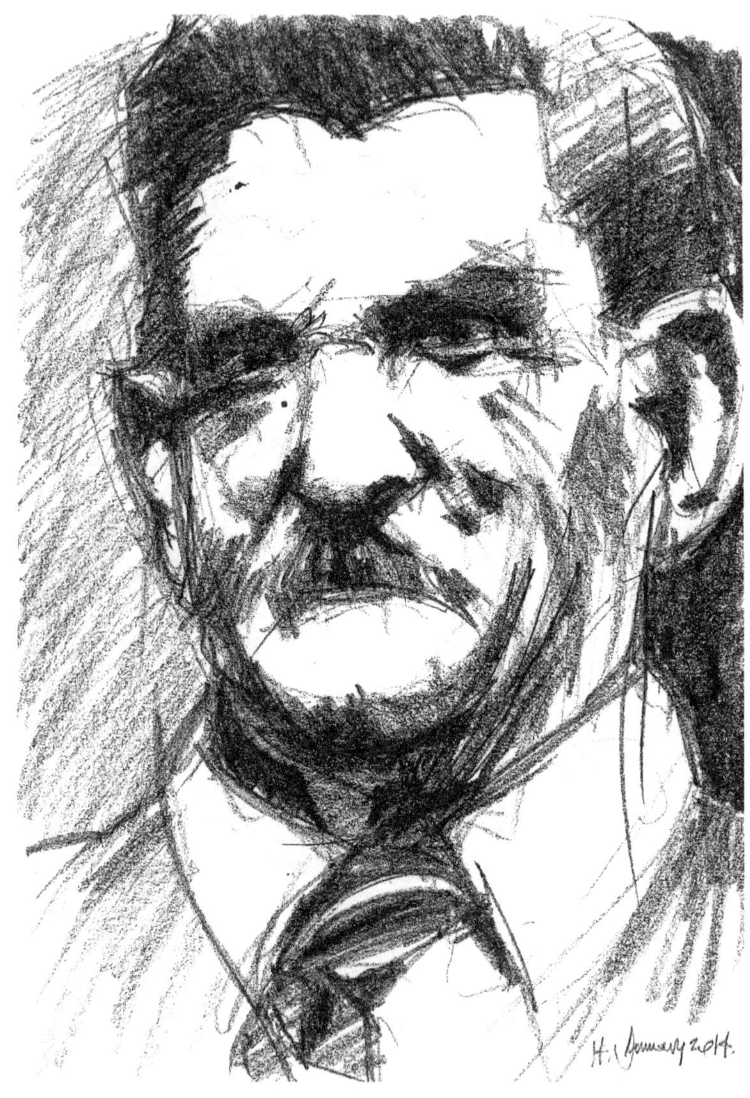

'MY GREAT GRANDFATHER, ROBERT HIGGENSON SNR.'
Block graphite on Cartridge Paper, 2014

ONCE MORE COMES CHRISTMAS

Once more comes Christmas
crashing on us in the rush
that's come to be expected.

Summer's wings are scarcely spread
when suddenly the longest day
has come and gone ...
A metaphor for life, really.

So spread our days
to skip before us,
spinning out of sight.

This year has seen our hares move on;
our hill un-grazed, to languish
in its sea of unchecked weeds ... and weeds
I do not wish, no more than might, do you.

The pretty golds and mauves
all come and gone; how fitting now the season ...
These Father Christmas seed heads in their stead.

I came here once to love you;
nurture and support through all these seasons;
cherish you and serve you come what may.
For what weeds grew, I do regret them –
and with this Christmas time, I'll clear some paths.

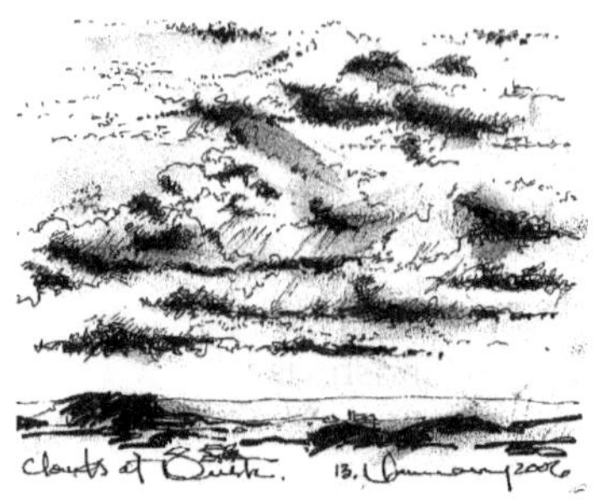

'CLOUDS AT DUSK'
Pen & wash on Arches Paper, 2006

OF LATE, AT NIGHT, OUR LANES

Of late, at night, our lanes themselves are bare
while neighbours hounds still bark their way
through life and seasons, day by day ...
Thus guarantee the absence of our hares:
once, great delights of summer, now dismay.

Another twelve months come and passed ...
Still yet another February, slips upon us
without one fanfare, leaving us non-plussed.
No more our joyful gambolling hares ... they're past;
reminders gone, to which we must adjust.

The year has seen no trace of summer's winding down:
as hot a prelude to this Day of Lovers ever felt ...
A Valentines designed to make all steam and melt
on our mountaintop of green-clad towns
where even dogs are silenced by such heat as forecasts spelt.
In spite of such discomforts, I still hold you dear
and wish you joyful Valentines, in all the best good cheer.

SEVENTEEN-SEVENTY OBSERVED

With melting-down of day across our bay,
this languid air exhales and holds its breath ...
If but an instant – vain though it might try
to hold day's pulse in check,
an impulse to inhale at length gives way ...

So breathe it does, the very bay to tremor
in this late day's holy speckled blaze ...
The curtains stir – the bougainvillea quiver.

Across the bay, the coastal sand-dunes haze –
lost to the gather of shimmering sea-alight,
whose mirrored rippling blinds and sears the eyes
as setting sun pours out – sparks waters to ignite ...
A brilliance, burning red and bright enough to daze.

Our atmosphere builds up as breezes gather ...
Tremble ... While on our Naked Bow, all sways
as dusk-bent stirrings herald in cool weather.

The setting sun at bay's rim, in that moment, flares ...
Ignites those far-flung ranges still in reach
and, near to hand, all water and its coastline fades
as mute, the arms of evening stretch
their fast embrace, to hold all in her shades.

Night settles in ... All pales ...
The stars and moorings' lights switch on ...
The bay breathes in – day's light is gone
and all on earth exhales.

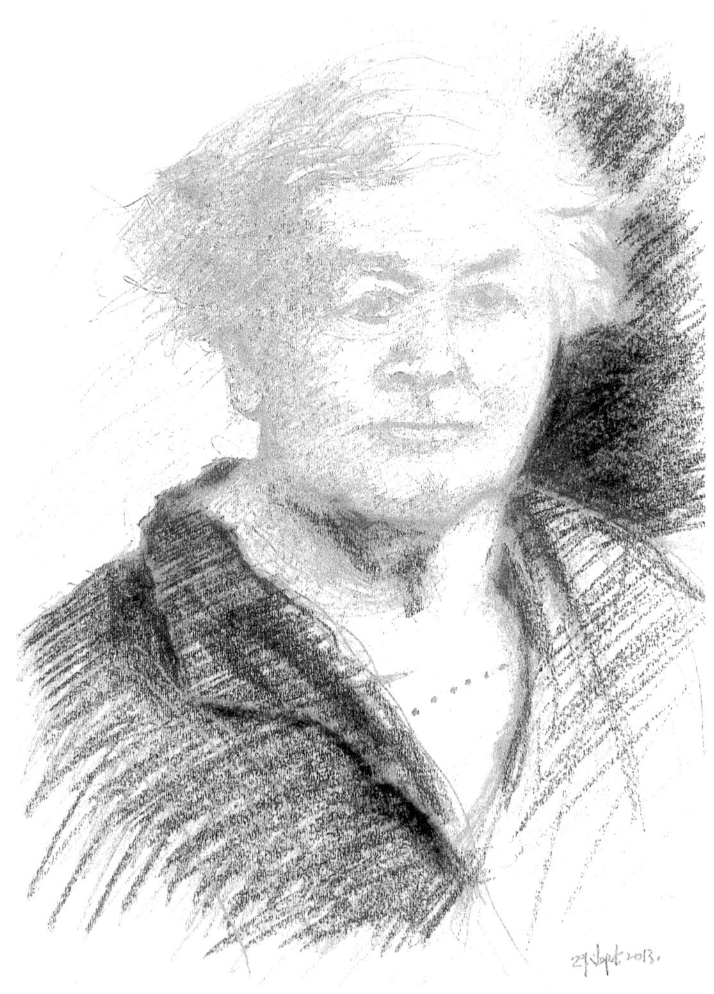

'MY GRANDFATHER'S BLOOD MOTHER, PERHAPS?'
Graphite block & conte crayon on Cartridge Paper, 2013

NOW SEVEN YEARS HAVE PASSED

Now seven years have passed, since first we sailed
our craft to plumb an unknown ocean's depth
(Such years as now reflect my own decade) ...
I had thought then, how with that step,
to claim some past ports' joys delayed ...
On far horizon's rim, lush lands were hailed.

So, hoisting anchor, sail we did ...
Our New World hove in sight
and to that promised shore, were led
our aspirations ... love come late.

So seven years have passed beneath our bow ...
Wayward beasts rose from our deepest myths;
though none of substance settled in our wake.
Our voyage destined, naught might mar
the purpose which those years could yoke
to strengthen our resolve, both then and now ...

Our harbour safe, protected, strong ...
Breakwaters shield our nurtured mooring,
while fo'c'sle bells, the years will ring
out clear: our odyssey unfolding.

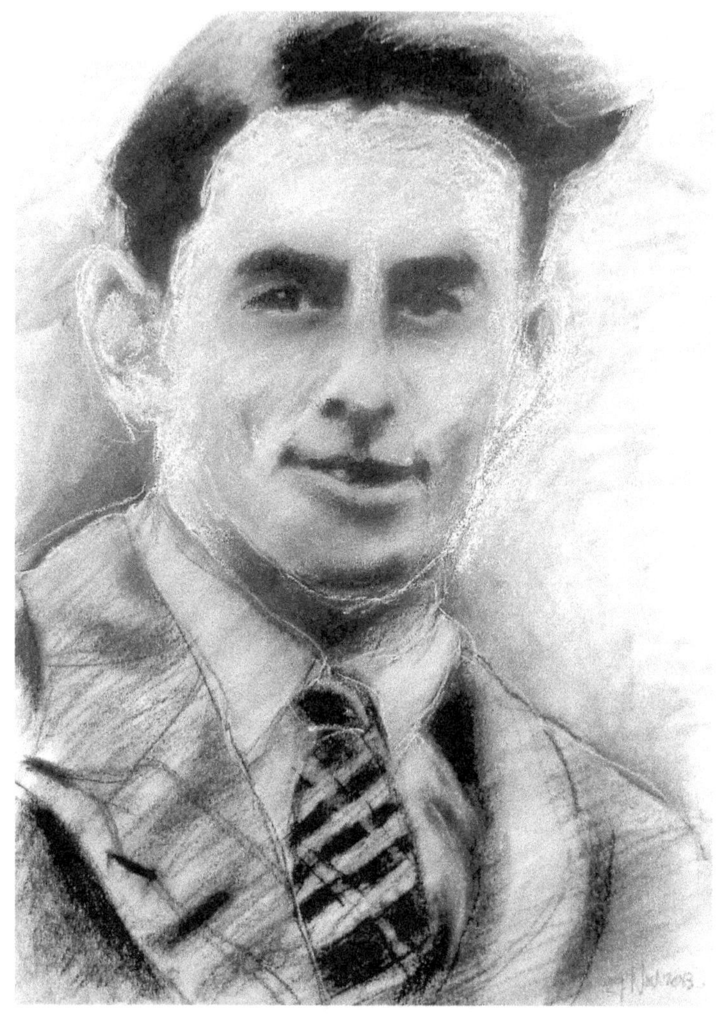

'MY FATHER AS A YOUNG MAN'
Conte crayon, chalk & compressed charcoal on Cartridge Paper, 2013

MY FATHER'S GHOST IS SLEEPING

My Father's ghost is sleeping on the stairs;
The attic air is musty with his heat.
    Heir to his chaptered blood
I recognise the scent of reason's breath
And navigate the corridors that bleed
This sap of singularity ... his heirs.

My Mother's brother's eyes gaze back from home
To burn me through the confines of the glass.
    With incandescent eye ...
From mirrors and shop windows as I pass,
He mocks all futile efforts made to flee
The stamp of blood fixed firm within the stone.

My Mother keeps her silence to herself;
Just hums and smiles discretely from the hearth.
    With patience and with love,
She stands aside ... to murmur through the breath
Contained within the stone, the stair, the blood,
That all is as it should be ... such is life.

Late afternoon's shaft filters through the slats;
Lights up each mote of dust upon the sill ...
    Illumined shards long-gone
Come present ... gather likewise, for us all –
Reminders of the blood stored in the stone ...
My Father's ghost is stirring, as he sleeps upon the stairs.

I WOULD, IF COULD, SING UNTO YOU ...

I would, if could, sing unto you a season
before the joy of innocence was lost;
before these times of binary-fostered reason
burnt bridges rationality had crossed.
I'd grant a season of much simpler times;
a season long before the web was spun ...
where self-promotion had no urgent walls to climb
and time was leisurely, no headlong race to run.

I'd sing you slow perfection's Christmas tidings:
a carol crafted lovingly with joy;
no settling for fast answers now abiding ...
a thoughtful softer patience to employ.
So as we move now through another Season,
let's aim for balance from this fledgeling reason.

(A Shakespearean sonnet)

AND YET AGAIN, A HEAT WAVE

And yet again, a heat wave comes
to summon up the day of Lovers ...
Steam our nights and drive our days indoors.

Even on our tempered Range enclave,
bright Mercury rises up his tube, to hover ...
Suck up humidity, with temperatures that soar.

These past two years, our hill, the hares have fled ...
We blamed the neighbours hounds
whose baying simply chased our hares, who sped

And so, we've missed their daily gambolling flights
their lazing on our hill; their bounds –
seen only now, along dark lanes by night ...

Small miracle! ... This summer's seen our hares retrace
their steps in boldness – claim our hill
to gently bless it by their grace ...

A sign that good things never travel far ...
though hid from sight, they're with us still –
and nor shall time or absence mar
the force which urges us combine
in every day, with Valentine.

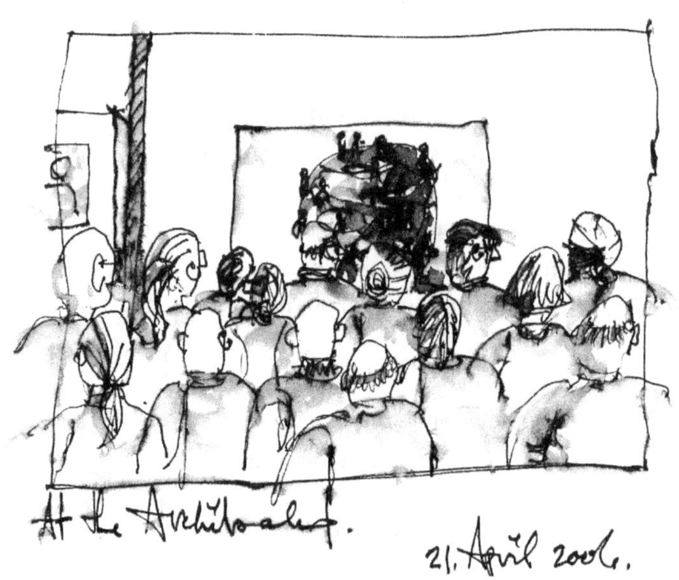

'AT THE ARCHIBALD, 2006'
Rollerball & wash on Arches Paper, 2006

THERE WAS A TIME THE HEAVENS ...

There was a time the heavens turned and shifted –
The stars changed order, constellations moved ...
Across our skies, raised sextants traced their passage.

Through these eight years, the sands of time have sifted;
Marked grain by grain, our journey as we roved
To set our sails and sights on one last anchorage ...
Safe harbour in a New World glimpsed afar.

The years have flown since that first brave embarkment,
With compass set and caution cast to winds
Which carried us, our craft, to this safe haven

Where storm surge abates, in lee of deep content ...
And were there things our sailor might rescind,
He'd answer, 'There is naught that I can fathom,
Nor that I'd change or swap for any reason,
As I set in sight the wake of your Pole Star.'

A WITCHY POEM FOR MADISON

'Hubble (not the telescope),
Bubble, toil and trouble
Cauldron boil and cauldron bubble ...
Where sleeps our Mac tonight?'
Or summat like that, Macbeth's three witches
Chanted ... or were they five?

Now, they were creepy –
Led Macbeth and worrisome wifey
Quite astray, they did ...
And trees? Talk about trees! ...
Did you ever see woods walking?

Well, woods were what quite finished them,
Come their sorry ends ...
And everyone's quite favourite bard –
Young Shakespeare of the frothy collar,
Knew how to spin a yarn of that.

Wisemen ... and Wise-women ... young or old
Could learn a thing or three,
The way Bard Willie set them down.

(For seven-year old Madison Wiseman ...
A response to her prize-winning school poem regarding witches.)

CHRISTMAS COMES BUT ONCE A YEAR

Christmas comes but once a year.
Again it's caught me unawares ...
I'd thought it safe to say, 'It's near'
then muse ahead, what words to share ...
but time fooled me, for suddenly it's here!

Yes, suddenly The Day is here.
I'd thought once more, some verse to write
to hail this Season loud and clear
and sing sweet greetings – nothing trite –
to fill your Christmas morn with cheer ...

Yes, fill your Christmas morn with cheer.
Instead, I pour this drivel out
as doggerel, whose form I fear
and scorn in others' word-some bouts,
which warrant not the term, sincere.

But Christmas does come once a year
and though our Range dawn bright or drear,
my love for you is always here.
Your presence in my life is dear ...
and near to me, my heart you cheer.

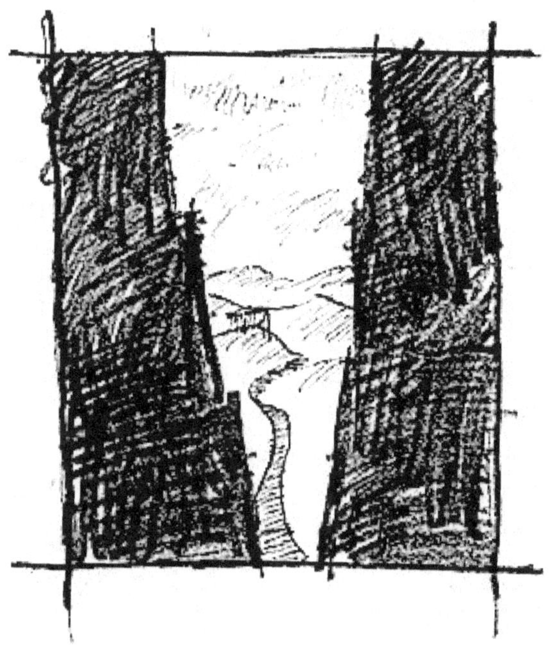

'RAVINE'
Pencil Notebook Study for screenprint, 1979

I KNOW THAT SOMEWHERE OUT THERE

I know that somewhere out there, roams our hare.
He's followed us at this time through the years,
to mark each exit of the summer's season.
Now Eros draws his bow to loose his flight,
Tipped with a barb to render sense or reason
mute, nullified ... a slave to all that's fair
and loveliest ... to follow day and night,
without a qualm, without a doubt, bereft of fears.

The foliage gracing half our slope has flourished.
Dandelions stand their ground on what remains ...
Though hid from us, I've marked our hare's quick passage
when on odd occasions, he's caught unawares.
Now autumn moves to bear her full fruit homeward,
Bold Eros girds his bow and loving quiver ...
Shafts never emptied, for his aim is true.

It's Valentine's ... and once again for asking,
'Will you love me simply, just as I love you?'

WE DWELL IN THE HOUR OF PERFIDY

We dwell in the hour of perfidy ...
of smiling mouth and shielded eye;
of singular ambition spent
for the season politic ...
subversion's lie.

Old bodkin's friend, well-armed and girt
with promise and the well-plied lie ...
whose honeyed lips drip the garden's kiss,
as waiting surrogates stand by
the doors to opportunity and power.

No hallowed halls so reeked of trust
abandoned to the must and dust,
ambition laid so thickly on their walls.

We dwell in the hours of perfidy and greed …
to turn our backs on empathy and need,
while dreams of reason politic
with binary intent,
all other truths belie.

Here, in unseen quarters of the world,
Orwellian drum-rolls round the hour,
mark the beating of a culture spent …
and passing of intelligence lament
with Huxley's breath descending down its days.

Narcissi bloom beside each stream
to nod their heads in discourse self-contained …
while busy fingers thumb each screen,
mute-slavish to a culture rent by social discourse –
slow advents to anarchy in reason.

'Mere treachery!' the traitors cry, lulling us to sleep;
while in the glow of evening screens,
by every other option urged to dreams
of avarice and winning come what may …
we trade our minds.

In perfidies we thrive and throng,
as each new trinket croons the song
distraction needs to guarantee our slumber.

THE CROW ('CORVUS MULTIFACETUS')

Stark, dark and sometimes sonorous: The Crow –
harshly the grumble, gently to chuckle and mutter;
funereal, to strut and stride about his stage
(for all the world's his own to fill) ...
wherein to bleat and caw his way through life.

For want of song, chants dolorous complaint
with studied reverence ... to terminate each sermon
with considered, drawn-out 'Aaaaawww!'
Whereon, forgetting what he really meant to say,
he'll start again to recommence his caw.

Occasionally, he'll toss sardonic humour in
to bounce, hop, jump and skip awhile
(but not too much, mind you) ...
we must maintain our gravitas
with solemnity in undertaker roles.

When all is done, he'll settle softly with his mate
to chat together, rest awhile ... to chuckle
at her jokes and 'Chuk-Chuk' oh so gently
in her dark mysterious ear.

The raven, crow, the rook and jackdaw
abide the wide world over and knock
at poets' doors in dead of night ...
there, 'Nevermore!' to whisper, through the confines
of the dark and mock the tossing sleeper in his plight.

They feast on death about the roadsides;
leave no blood-bright corpse unturned ...
cadavers grant them nourishment and joy.
They scorn unwary drivers, as they set about their meal
reluctant to break from their carrion zeal.

Their reputation tarnished by the prejudice of myth,
they bear the burden lodging in their eye ...
with steady glare, they challenge all to fear
death's chill and ready doom, gazed down
from lonely fenceposts, or the carapace of tombs.

In spite of all the bad-press, they're a most congenial lot
when gathered round in numbers of their own.
Omnivorous they are in truth, living simply on their wits,
whilst taking care in sharing family chores.

They're clever and resourceful, quite adept at forging tools;
intelligent ... as mimics, highly skilled.
They're family people, dedicated fully to their task
while sharing through their cross-talk, dawn to dusk.

So look upon them softly, as you take their chatter in ...
They're not the stark dark harbingers of doom.
They're simply nature's cleaners, in pursuit of nature's awe –
to quantify her beauty with their starkly clarion caw.

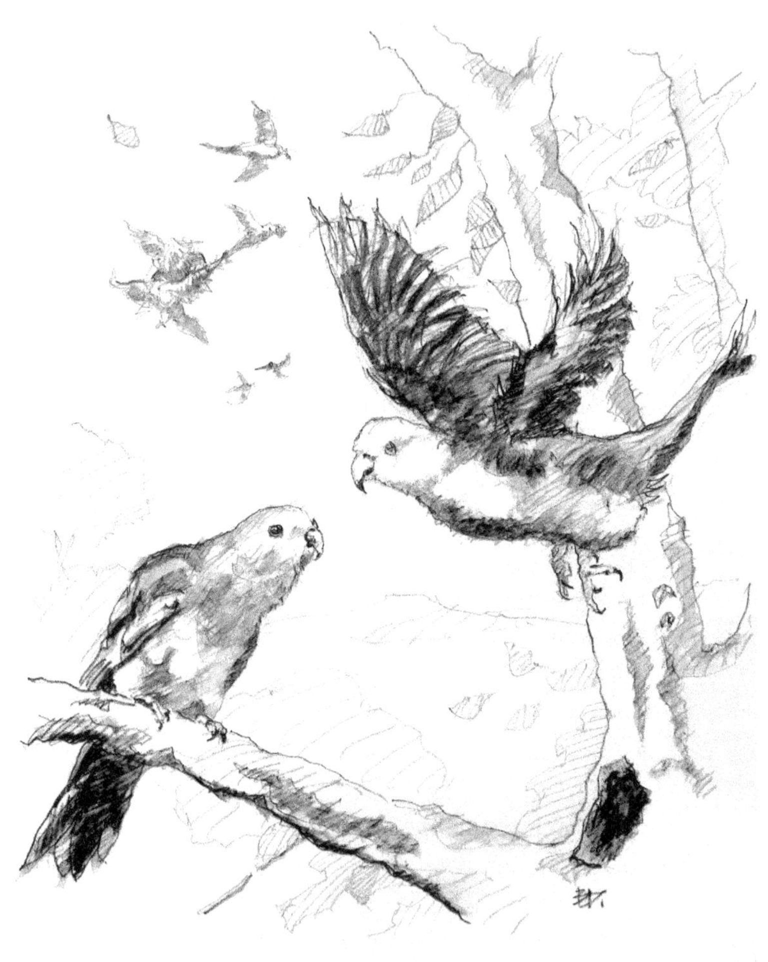

'KING PARROTS, MONTVILLE'
Aquarelle graphite pencil with wash on Cartridge Paper, 2017

WE NESTLED IN SAFE WATERS ...

We nestled in safe waters;
cast our anchor in the lee
of cloud-capped mountains ...
in this now, one ninth year's setting
bravely forth upon our voyage,
as we cast our fates forth to the beckoning sea.

We safe-moored, rose up to settle
on these mist-topped, rolling heights
of lush green ranges, where buffeted
by all the fluxing winds of seasons,
we've kept our home fires stoked
and glowing warmly round our love ...

Here shelters our companionship
with comforts of our music,
our books, our art – all nurtured
by the muse who reigns here on this verdant range –
sustaining souls with nourishment
not found within the gushing rush of heady coastal plains.

From these lush and rolling heights
we might survey the sea which bore us
(when clouds and mist lift, to permit one such).
Though in one full day, we ramble
through most-every other season,
change wardrobe up or down at every turn ...

Lodged within the cloud-swept ramparts
of this eyrie resting safely here upon our rolling range,
there is nothing I would alter
as we lock our life craft's hatches,
to batter-down, for all that life might throw ...
I set forth once like Columbus,
sailing for a fabled New World,
to find it in this haven of your heart.

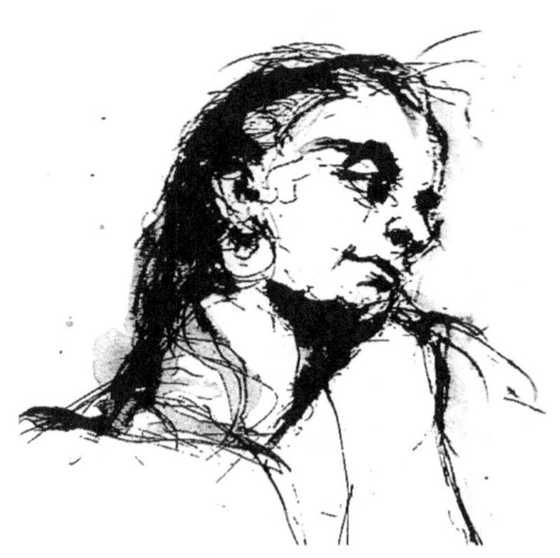

'HEAD OF A WOMAN' Detail
Rollerball & wash on Arches Paper, 2009

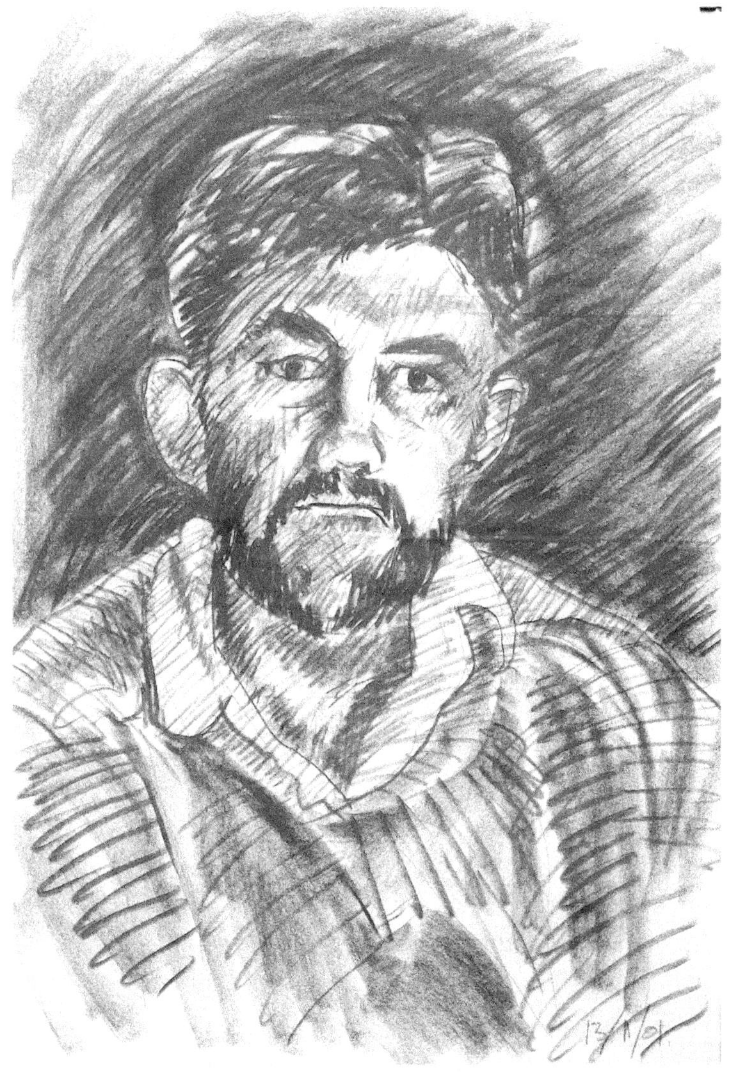

'FRANK'

Compressed charcoal on Newsprint, 2001

THE BRUSHES AND THE PENS,
ARE STILL AND SILENT ...

The brushes and the pens, are still and silent now.
The pastels and the chalks are fast asleep –
All hue and cry of pencils, rendered mute.

No more, the gleeful gestures of this fertile mind –
The florid fancies of his inward eye, no more
To grace the reams of papers gathered here.

The mimic and the wit, have had their day –
The lightfast humour vented, soon would fade
And dusk come down to dim where daylight glowed.

But still the reel keeps turning, while the stories flicker on
And ever in the background, ring the songs
Of Louii, Frankie, Tony, Ella – every jazz-bound Great.

Bright stars in heaven now claim him as their own ...
The myriad of loves he held, pursued him to the end
And left their imprint here for all to see – how fevered
Burnt this candle, through its much too, far short life.

(IN MEMORIAM, FRANK MOFFATT ... Children's book illustrator,
artist and writer, best friend ... ardent lover of all things bookish,
cinematic and theatrical, along with the jazz greats ... mimic and dry humorist,
quiet philosopher and modest wit ... truly, Ein Mensch.)

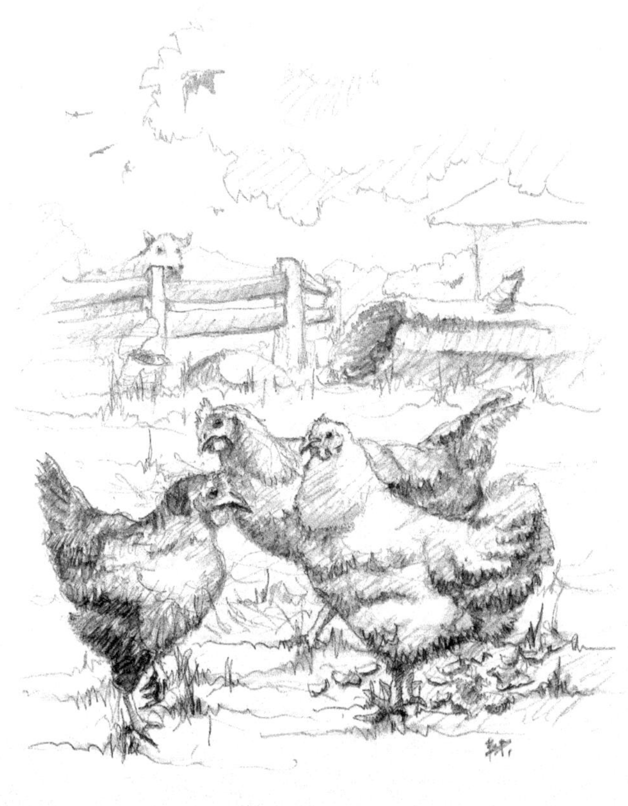

'HAPPY CHOOKS: THREE FRIENDS''
Aquarelle graphite pencil with wash on Cartridge Paper, 2017

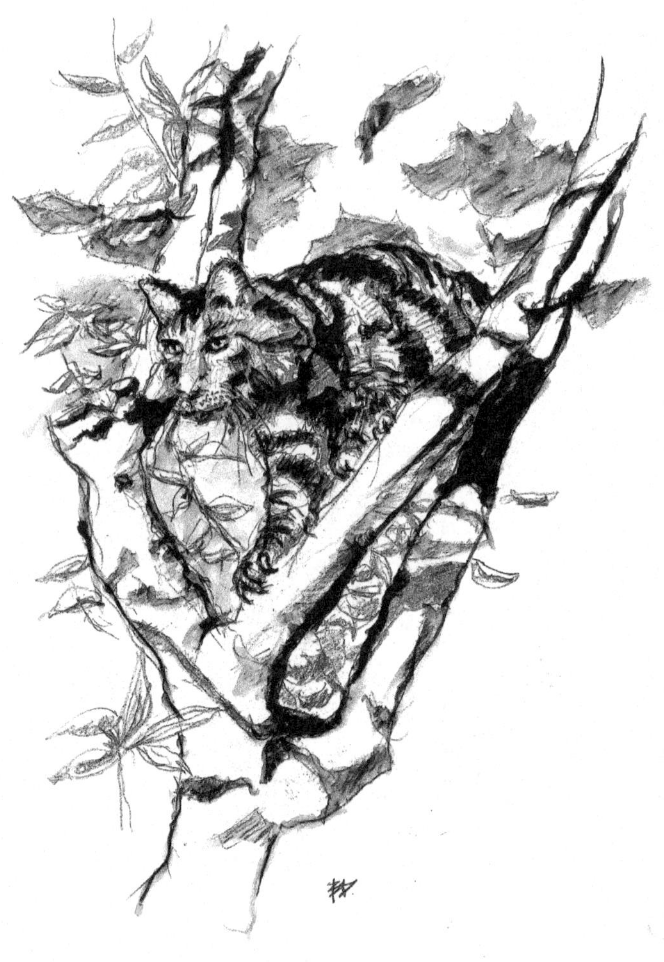

'MAX, THE CAT'
Aquarelle graphite pencil with wash on Cartridge Paper, 2017

ONCE MORE, I FIND I'M TAKEN BY SURPRISE

Once more, I find I'm taken by surprise
as Christmas rushed in quickly, once again.
We've been so busy watching cloudless skies,
I'd overlooked the need to prime my pen
whilst wondering if it would rain ... and when.

It will rain sometime; question is, Just when?
This year we need it more than we have most,
with weathers taking on a nasty spin ...
where fires rage; homes, animals, are lost;
while politicians juggle all their costs

With scant regard for common people's costs ...
where smoke and mirrors cloud the light of day;
obscure the rights and liberties fast lost
and still, the droughts and fires, come what may.
The best that they can offer is to pray.

In spite of dire disaster, I would pray
you health and happiness, for all our years ...
surmount all obstacles to come our way,
bring light of hope to banish any fears
while Christmas times ring joys so loud and clear.

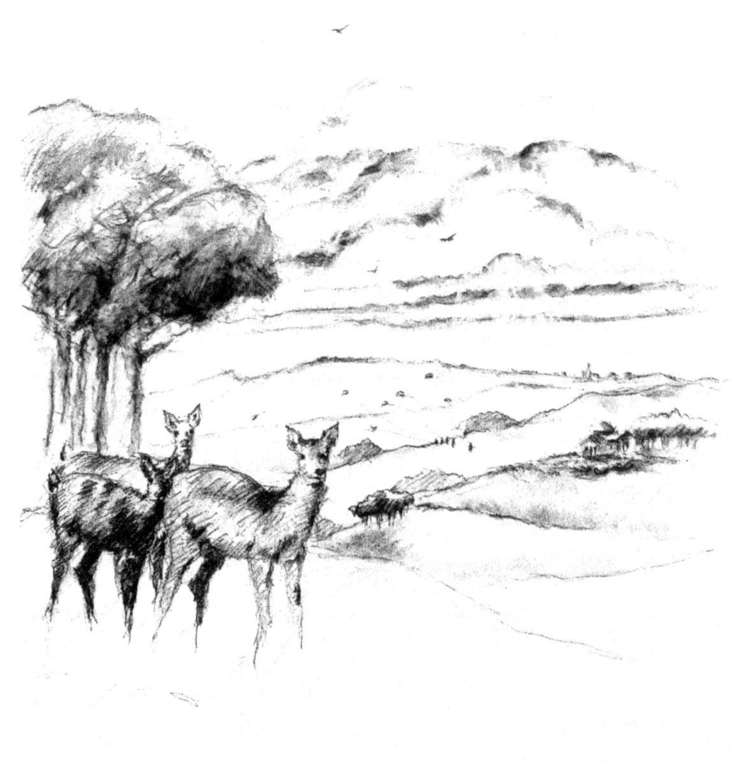

'RICHMOND HILL, 1975'
Notebook sketch, Aquarelle graphite & wash, recalled 2020

BRIGHT AND SHINING ...

Bright and shining was the cup she bore
But its bowl wore a tarnish under.
Glowing and soft was the skin she wore
To strike him with awe and wonder.
And full-well he knew, that when she left
The world that he knew would soon be cleft,
Leaving his years rent asunder.

Silken and soft was the cloth she wove
And its threads held his undoing.
True and constant the heart he gave,
All other claims eschewing.
In time, time flew and a distance leapt
Into the space that his pulse had swept
Far from the other's knowing.

Years, then decades, would at length run on
While the weft would become unravelled –
The dream once dreamed, now a dream long gone
With its byways no longer travelled ...
Until all that remained was an afternoon claimed
Where the red deer stood still out on Richmond Hill
And while the boys' kites and hawks were high flying –
And a gentle caress sent in motion, the test
When the slow wheels of fate were set turning.

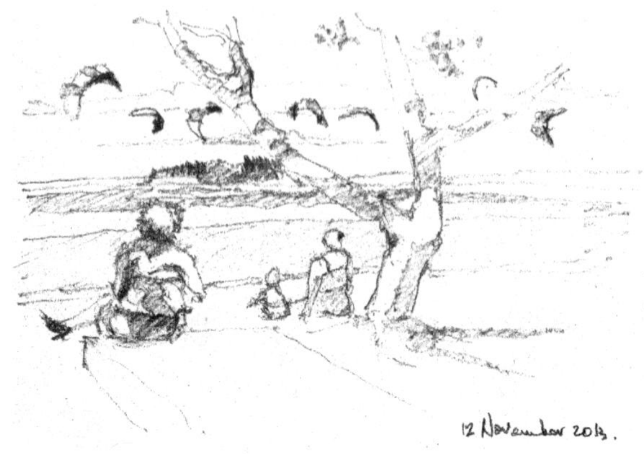

'HIGH-FLYERS AT COTTON TREE'
Aquarelle pencil notebook sketch, 2013

THERE CAME A TIME ...

There came a time when man was sent to trial ...
For squandered excess, too long fuelled his greed;
Forever wrapped his days in blind denial.

A pestilence born, some would say, from vials:
The virus spread its spawned, almighty seeds
To bring a time when man was brought to trial.

Time's hands long-chasing midnight on earth's dial
As many still pretended 'There's no need.' ...
Forever wrapping ways in blind denial.

Man's growth in numbers challenged reason's cavel;
Consumption's wants, the basis for their creed ...
So came a time when all was put on trial.

The spreading of the pathogen went viral
When magnified by public media's speed;
All rationale lost in some blind denials.

With commonsense fast lost, the cry 'Survival!'
Rebounded through most shopping malls to feed
New times where courtesies were put to trial.

As weeks turned into months beyond retrieval,
Mortalities mount higher and exceed
All figures leaders gauged, in their denials.

Then finally, amidst the wreckage global,
Humanity took stock and sought to heed
The lessons learnt when they were sent to trial ...
Forever wrapped in dreams of blind denial.

(An extended villanelle,
in tribute to the global pandemic of 2020:
Covid 19 ... The Corona Virus)

A LOCKDOWN SONNET

Another day of musing what to do next
Became the battlecry across the land ...
With only so much news that one might text,
This isolation's getting out of hand.
The boredom and the ennui are so deadly
And jigsaw sellers watch their profits grow;
All brief encounters seen as most ungodly ...
The social web, its slipstream in full flow.

What will it take to take us back to normal?
Will normal ever be the norm again?
Is it likely that this thing could have a sequel?
Are we always on the knife-edge until then?
What made us think that we could rule this planet?
We're simply pawns in mortal roles, God dammit!

A Shakespearean sonnet
to the lockdown provisions of Covid 19
during the pandemic of 2020)

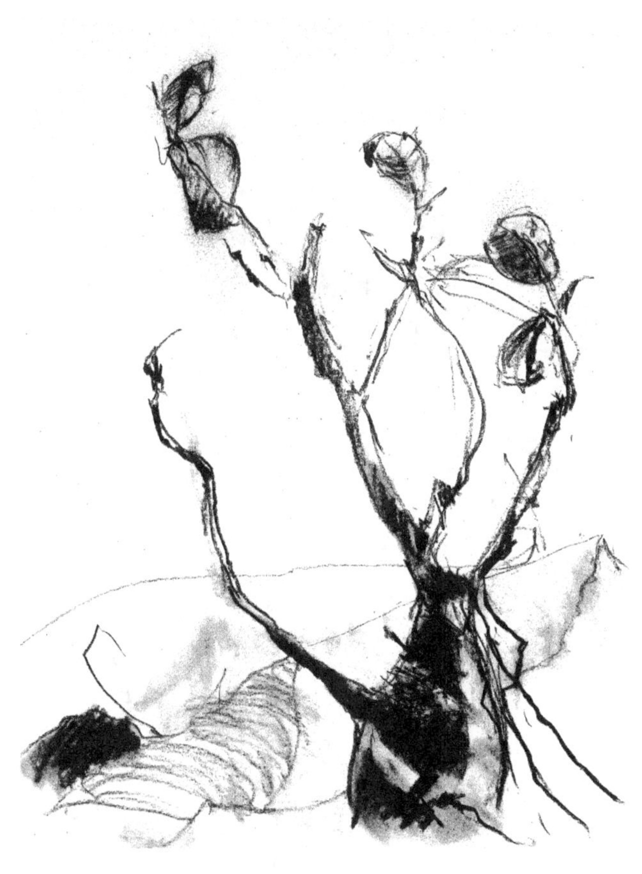

'STRUGGLING PLANT AT HERVEY BAY'
Notebook sketch with charcoal pencil, 2015

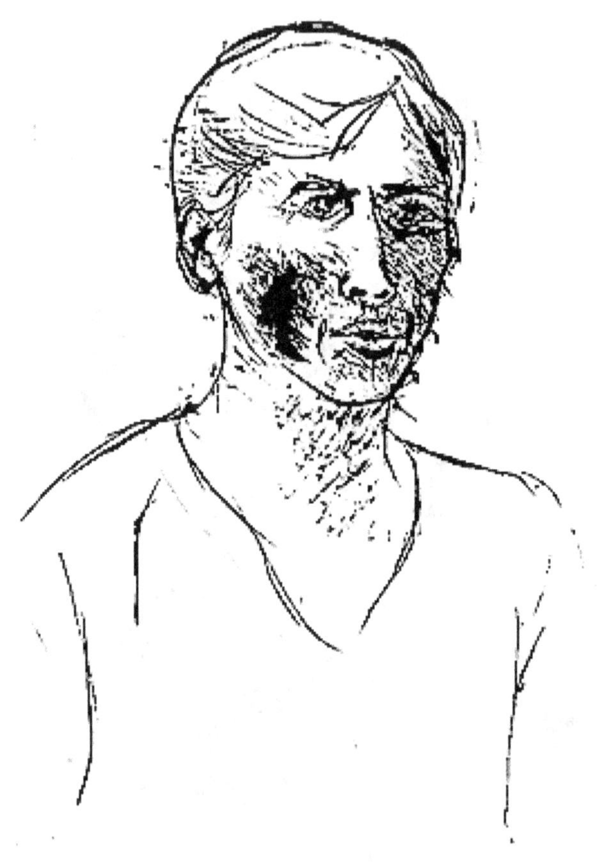

'ANOTHER SELF PORTRAIT, 1983'
Quill liner & Indian ink on Fabriano Paper.